Ride Y

GW01019505

Contents

How to use this guide

The Ride Your Bike guides are designed for riders of all levels: from complete novices and those with a little experience to people who have been cycling all their lives.

Chapter 1 aims to whet the appetite for the area covered by the guide. As well as general information about the geological character and history of the region, places of interest are identified and described.

Chapter 2 provides important basic information on preparing yourself and your bike before a ride, getting to the start of a route, navigation skills, as well as advice on safety and emergencies.

If you would like to know more about bikes, equipment, repair and maintenance and travelling further afield into Europe and the rest of the world, *Mountain Biking, The Bike Book* and *Fix Your Bike* are published by Haynes and are available from all good bike and bookshops.

A locator map is included on pages 4-5 for easy identification of rides in your area. The ride facts chart at the back of the guide is designed to provide key information 'at a glance' to make selecting a ride that suits your mood, energy level and degree of expertise simple and quick.

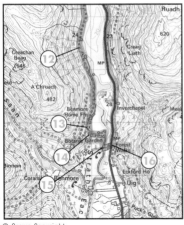
© Crown Copyright

The guide contains 18 rides graded easy, medium and difficult.

Easy rides are for novices, families with young children and for people who are getting back into riding after a gap. They are relatively short and use good surfaces such as dismantled railways. You don't need any expertise to do these rides just the enthusiasm to get out there.

Medium rides are a little more challenging in terms of distance and terrain. If you have done all the easy routes, have built up some confidence and mastered the basic trail techniques try one of the shorter routes in this category. You will soon feel able to try the rest. Check through the directions to alert yourself to anything you may not be able to manage.

Difficult rides are for the experienced mountain biker and demand a good command of trail techniques, fitness and more than a dash of courage. They are exciting and challenging and great fun. Make sure you and your bike are in good shape before you contemplate a difficult route: they often go into remote areas and use challenging terrain.

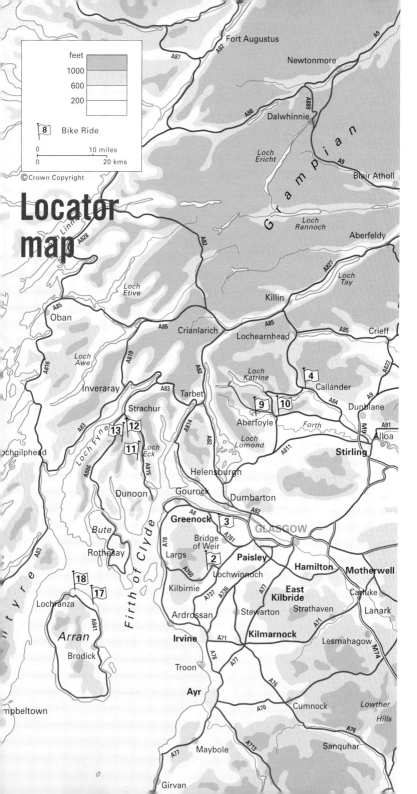

Locator map

feet
1000
600
200

🏴 8 Bike Ride

0 ——— 10 miles
0 ——— 20 kms

©Crown Copyright

Fort Augustus
A87
A82
Newtonmore
A86
A889
Dalwhinnie
Loch Ericht
Loch Linnhe
A828
Loch Etive
Grampian
Loch Rannoch
A9
Blair Atholl
Aberfeldy
A82
A827
Loch Tay
Killin
Oban
A85
Crianlarich
Lochearnhead
A85
Crieff
A822
Loch Awe
A85
A819
Loch Katrine
4 Callander
A84
Dunblane
A9
A91
Inveraray
A83
Tarbet
9 10
Aberfoyle
Forth
Alloa
Strachur
A814
Loch Lomond
A811
Stirling
M9
13 12
Loch Fyne
11
Loch Eck
A815
A82
Helensburgh
A85
chgilphead
A886
Dunoon
Gourock
Dumbarton
A8
A82
GLASGOW
Bute
Greenock
3
A761
Rothesay
A78
Bridge of Weir
Largs
2
Paisley
Hamilton
Motherwell
Lochwinnoch
A760
Kilbirnie
A737
A736
East Kilbride
Strathaven
Carluke
18
17
Ardrossan
Stewarton
A77
Lanark
Lochranza
A841
Irvine
A71
Kilmarnock
A71
Lesmahagow
M74
Arran
Troon
A78
A77
Brodick
A76
mpbeltown
Ayr
A70
Cumnock
Lowther Hills
A76
A77
Maybole
A713
Sanquhar
Girvan

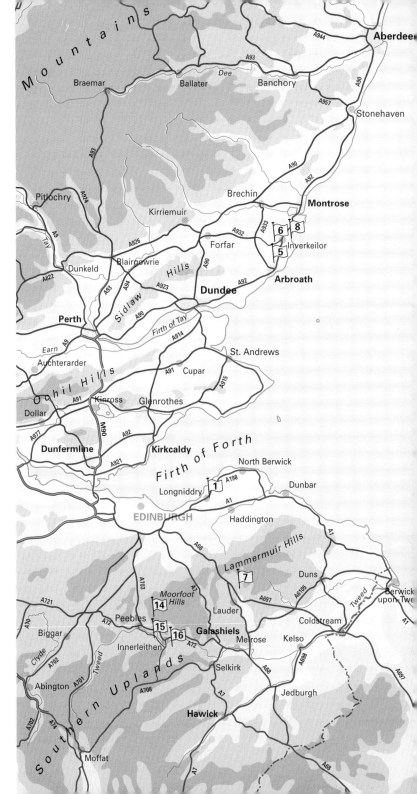

Chapter 1: Angus and the Highland Fringe

ABOUT ONE THIRD OF ANGUS is highland country, the northern skyline dominated by the Grampian Mountains, but the south-east is definitely lowland, highly agricultural and subject to intensive land use. Huge bales of straw awaiting removal from the field cast long shadows as the sun sets at harvest time, whilst throughout the year you will see all manner of crops at various stages of growth. The number of true off-road mountain-biking routes are very limited, but country lanes, known and used for the greater part only by the locals, provide relaxing riding in a landscape of soft fruits, grain, potatoes and, of course, beef cattle. For great distances a short row of cottages or a couple of steadings adjoining a farm are the only settlements.

Seabirds on the red sandstone of the Devil's Heid, Carlingheugh Bay, Arbroath

The other face of Angus is the off-shore oil industry; support vessels and the occasional drilling rig are often to be seen close by. And of course there is the fishing industry which survives remarkably well at Arbroath despite the decline all around the North Sea.

Loch Drunkie, near Achray Forest

Places to visit

Stirling, a university town, contains museums, an arts and leisure centre and the historic **Bannockburn Centre and Wallace Memorial** which is open from Easter to October. **Aberfoyle** is one of the destinations of the **Trossachs Trundler**, a 1950s bus service. The **Highland Boundary Fault Trail**, a 2–3 hour walking route begins at Aberfoyle and you can also visit the Forest Visitors Centre called David Marshall Lodge. Two trails for drivers are the **Trossachs Trail** and the **Achray Forest Drive**, for which you have to pay a toll. In **Arbroath**, to the east of the area, you can visit Arbroath Abbey, St Vigean's Church and the Celtic museum. The oldest British built warship, the frigate *Unicorn* is still afloat at **Dundee** which is worth a visit for the Mills Observatory, the Broughty Castle Museum, which houses displays on the history of whaling, and the Barrack Street Natural History Museum. There is also **Discovery Point** where **Scott of the Antarctic's** research ship, *Discovery*, is berthed, alongside a splendid exhibition. Outdoor pursuits including golf can be taken up at the world famous Carnoustie complex, Letham Grange and Monikie Country Park.

Rides in this area featured in the book: Callander to Strathyre, Smokin' Arbroath, Lunan Bay, Inverkeilor and the Lunan Water, Achray Forest and the Duke's Pass, Loch Ard

The Cowal Peninsula

A fungus which grows on sphagnum and is a delicacy for deer

So NEAR YET SO FAR: the Cowal peninsula has all the rugged grandeur of the 'other' Highlands farther north, but if you use one of the Clyde ferries it is only 50 kms (30 miles) from Glasgow. It is part of the mainland and you can drive to it if you wish. But there is something about a ferry journey that sets the scene for a totally different environment and you disembark into another world.

These mountains are actually part of the Highlands – the line runs from the Isle of Arran in a north-easterly direction through Aberfoyle to Stonehaven on the east coast – but most traffic misses these parts which have developed an atmosphere all of their own. Even some of the A roads are a single track with passing places, a characteristic usually reserved for the islands or the far north. You can almost touch the quiet.

The wildlife is a mixture of what you would expect in the Highlands, red and sika deer, eagles and the pine marten, plus Lowland regulars, such as roe deer, rabbits and weasels. The star of the show was an immaculate golden pheasant, seen by the author near Strachur. It wandered jauntily across the road, obviously having total faith in the skills of the onrushing biker. Once you get a feel for the place you will inevitably want to see more than the area covered by this guide and Cowal is worth a visit at any time of year.

Places to visit

Steamer cruising on the *Waverley, Saturn* or *The Second Snark* is available from April to October (check before going) departing from **Dunoon** which also has a visitor centre and limited tourist facilities. The Loch Eck Circuit goes through the grounds of the **Younger Botanic Garden** at Benmore which houses impressive trees, especially the giant Californian redwoods. More ornamental trees, shrubs and Scottish forestry can be seen at **Kilmun Arboretum**, Kilmun. Fine but tough walking territory can be found in the **Arrochar Alps**, north of Glen Croe including Ben Arthur, known as **the Cobbler**. The **European Sheep and Wool Centre** at the Drimsynie leisure centre, Lochgoilhead, is open from April to October. The centre also offers an opportunity to try the Scottish outdoor pursuit of **curling**. Pony trekking is available at the Carrow Centre in Lochgoilhead or at the Velvet Path Centre in Inellan.

The forest road from Glenshellish Farm into Glen Shellish

Rides in this area featured in the book: Glenshellish, Glen Branter, Loch Eck Circuit

Leithen Hopes and the eastern fringes of Glentress Forest, from a viewpoint on Wallace Hill

The Upper Tweed Valley and East Lothian

THE TWEED VALLEY has been renowned worldwide for its textiles for many years and it still is. But what has been neglected until recently is the sheer severity and beauty of the place. The hill farms still produce wool, but not as much as before, and many of the mills have closed, rationalised production or are now using a greater proportion of man-made fibres. However, this seems to have given the forestry a chance to expand its influence, creating new roads and tracks and even more opportunity to ride these splendid hills.

There are several old thoroughfares, such as the Minchmoor Road, the Thieves' Road, and drovers' routes south into England, but these are serious long-distance commitments. Meanwhile the forests of the Upper Tweed are challenges, every one, so do not underestimate them.

It is easy to bypass East Lothian as you hurry along the A1, but as soon as you turn off the Great North Road the attractive highly agricultural countryside and sprinkling of castles and fine houses tempt you to stay. It was here that turnips were first sown in drills, thereby solving the problem of feeding cattle in the winter, one of the innovations of the great Improvers who revolutionised agriculture in the 18th century.

Places to visit

Edinburgh is within good striking distance and its impressive and varied attractions probably need no introduction. The International Festival and the military tattoo take place in August. There is a wealth of historic sites to visit including **Dirleton Castle, Hailes Castle** near Haddington, **Tantallon Castle**, North Berwick and the stylish **Thirlestane Castle** at Lauder which has wonderfully decorated ceilings, a nursery preserved from **Victorian** times and a countryside exhibition. The **Museum of Flight** can be visited at East Fortune Airfield and, for an insight into the making of Scotland's most famous tipple, try the **Glenkinchie Distillery** at Pencaitland. **Sir Walter Scott** resided at Abbotsford, Melrose which is also interesting for **Melrose Abbey**, the motor museum and the Roman Trimuntian exhibition. Salmon and trout fishing can be arranged from **Peebles** which also has good tourist facilities for all the family. Gardening enthusiasts may want to visit the **Dawyck Botanic Garden**, and a specialist garden of the Royal Botanic Garden, Edinburgh is at Stobo.

Rides in this area featured in the book: Elibank, Cardrona, Glentress, Longniddry to Haddington, The Bermuda Triangle

The lower stretch of the Minchmoor Road doubling as the Southern Upland Way

Renfrewshire

O NCE THE INDUSTRIAL HEART OF SCOTLAND, supplying all manner of heavy industries on the Clyde with their raw materials, many of the hills and glens of Renfrew are becoming beautiful countryside again. No doubt the locals would welcome many more jobs, and they may well come in time, but meanwhile the old railways have been converted to excellent leisure facilities which are well used and a good means of travelling about in what is still a busy area.

Barr Loch, Lochwinnoch, a very quiet spot viewed from the railway

The railway rides are as much a lesson in industrial archaeology and current reclamation techniques as a trip through splendid countryside and for anyone with any sort of background in heavy engineering absolutely fascinating. You will see grandfathers escorting the bairns along them, no doubt regaling them with tales of the past. But with the speed that the vegetation is claiming the country back you will understand any difficulty the wee ones may have in believing the stories.

Places to visit

Dalgarven Mill at Kilwinning is a working flour mill undergoing restoration. The mill also has a country life exhibition and a Scottish costume collection. **Eglinton Country Park**, also near Kilwinning, hosts craft fairs in the winter. There is also a small cycle track, an adventure playground and good walks. Castle Semple visitor centre is sited in the **Clyde Muirshiel Regional Park** where dinghy sailing, canoeing and rowing are on offer. At the **Castle Semple Nature Reserve** you can go bird watching and obtain information about the local bird life. On the coast, Irvine has a **Robert Burns** museum, a maritime museum, the Magnum leisure complex providing many sports facilities from racket sports to an ice rink. And, of course, there is the beach. **Glasgow** is within a half-hour drive of the area and, among other attractions, the open top bus tour of the city is highly recommended.

The railway path rich in summer vegetation, Bridge of Weir

Rides in this area featured in the book: Lochwinnoch, Bridge of Weir

The Isle of Arran

T HE ISLE OF ARRAN has been described as Scotland in miniature, and not without just cause, but as you look seaward from the ferry and see the classic silhouette of a Scottish island any doubts about its nature will be dispelled immediately. When you get there, you enter a different world. Much of the roadside herbage looks as if it has escaped from a domestic garden, the dense verges of montbretia being a stunning example. There are big hills, especially in the north, but a gentle coastal road takes you to them and the start of the two rides graded 'difficult'.

In Lochranza, the road runs right beside the beach.

In fact, there is no other way to get there. You can amalgamate them into a figure of eight and ride back to the ferry the same day, but this is not recommended unless you are very fit and very competent.

The pace is slower on Arran than on the mainland and there is much to see and enjoy: like the red deer on the Lochranza golf course first thing in the morning and yet another cave where Robert the Bruce met that spider, near Blackwaterfoot on the western seaboard. Take your time, enjoy the wildlife and the whole island, go first for a weekend, then go back again to drink in the atmosphere. You are almost certain to make friends, human or otherwise, who will compel your return.

Places to visit

The gardens and country park of **Brodick Castle** are open from Easter to October, as is the **Isle of Arran Heritage Museum** at Brodick. The ancient ruins of Kildonan Castle stand above Brodick Bay. The 400-year-old **Lochranza Castle** can be visited to the north of the island and there are a wealth of cairns such as **Kilpatrick Dun**, a Bronze Age ring cairn, as well as standing stones including the **Machrie Moor** standing stones and the **Auchgallon Stone Circle**. Recreational pursuits include paragliding, pony trekking and paintball tournaments. You can go on a Falco wildlife tour or take a cruise in the waters surrounding the isle.

Downhill to Lochranza

Rides in this area featured in the book: Fallen Rocks, Cock of Arran

Local amenities: contacts

For up-to-date information about accommodation (including a booking service), places to visit, public transport timetables and local events Tourist Information Centres offer an excellent service. See pages 18-19 for their location. Also given below are a few cycle hire companies although the local Information Centres will have the most up-to-date information on where to hire bicycles. Bike shops are also included where they exist close to the routes in this guide.

Tourist Information Centres

*Aberfoyle
Main Street, Aberfoyle, Perthshire
Tel: 01877 382352

Arbroath
Market Place, Arbroath, Angus DD11 1HR
Tel: 01241 872609

Brodick (Arran)
The Pier, Brodick, Isle of Arran KA27 8AU
Tel: 01770 302140

*Callander
Rob Roy and Trossachs Visitor Centre,
Ancaster Square, Callander, Perthshire
FK17 8ED (closed in Jan and Feb, Mon-Fri)
Tel: 01877 330342 Fax: 01877 330784

Dundee
4 City Square, Dundee DD1 3BA
Tel: 01382 434664 Fax: 01382 434665

Dunoon
7 Alexandra Parade, Dunoon, Argyll PA23 8AB
Tel: 01369 703785 Fax: 01369 706085

Glasgow
Tourist Information Desk, Glasgow
Airport, Paisley PA3 2FT
Tel: 0141 848 4440

Irvine
New Street, Irvine, Ayrshire KA12 8BB
Tel: 01294 313886

*Melrose
Abbey House, Abbey Street, Melrose,
Roxburghshire TD6 9LG
Tel: 01896 822555

North Berwick
Quality Street, North Berwick,
East Lothian EH39 4HJ
Tel: 01620 892197

Peebles
Chambers Institute, High Street,
Peebles EH45 8AG
Tel: 01721 720138

Stirling
41 Dumbarton Road, Stirling FJ8 2QQ
Tel: 01786 475019 Fax: 01786 471301
* not open all year

Ferry Operators

Caledonian MacBrayne, Hebridean and Clyde ferries

For Glenshellish, Glenbranter and Loch Eck Circuit contact: Gourock,
Tel: 01475 650100 Fax: 01475 637607
For Fallen Rocks and the Cock of Arran contact: Ardrossan, Tel: 01294 463470 and for the return journey contact: Brodick (Arran), Tel: 01770 302166

Western Ferries, Clyde/Argyll ferry

For Glenshellish, Glenbranter and Loch Eck Circuit contact: Dunoon,
Tel: 01369 704452 Fax: 01369 706020

Scottish Countryside Calendar

The details below are important considerations for the mountain biker, both from a personal safety and environmental point of view. It also shows consideration for the estate which manages the moors so well.

Red deer stalking

The open season for culling red deer stags is from 1 July–20 October; for hinds from 21 October–15 February. However the most critical time is generally from mid-August to mid-October.

Lambing

The exact time of hill lambing in Scotland varies according to the area, but is generally between mid-April and the end of May. Do not cause ewes in lamb to run under any circumstances.

Grouse shooting

The grouse shooting season runs from 12 August–10 December, with most shoots taking place during the earlier part of that period.

Nesting

Ground nesting birds on moorland can be very vulnerable to disturbance, especially whilst establishing nesting territories. Take particular care at nesting time, mid-April to the end of June, to allow the birds to nest and hatch successfully.

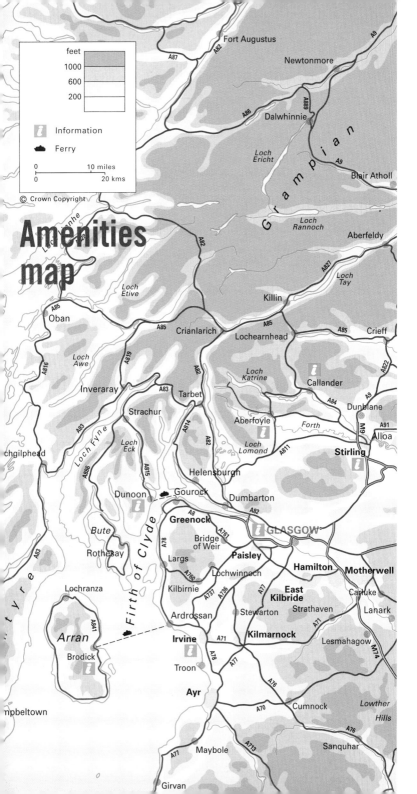

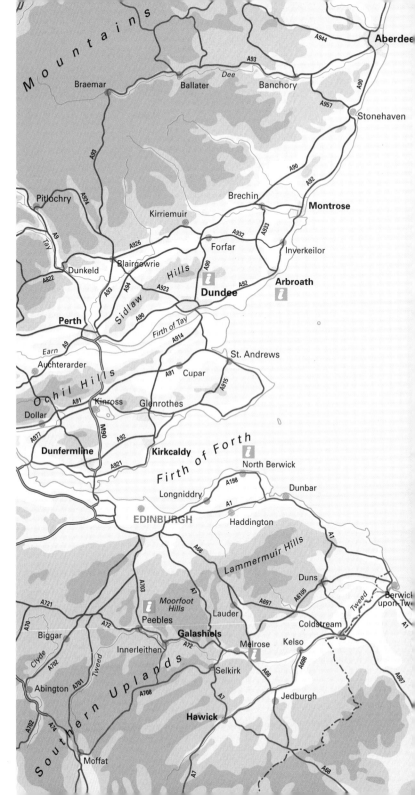

The glen of the
Earnscleugh Burn

Weather and seasons

Surfaces

As soon as you begin to ride off-road regularly, it will become obvious that some surfaces tolerate water and dampness better than others because they have fewer holes, fewer boggy sections and better drainage. Forest roads, converted railways and stony byways come into this category and can be ridden at any time of the year without fear of damage.

At the other end of the scale are the peat trails and sandstone moorland mixes, soft sensitive surfaces which are really only suitable for riding when bone dry or frozen solid. These are best avoided in springtime when any passage, wheels or feet, will leave a mark.

Water can have a disastrous effect on trails of any type, but more so on those without any surfacing. Even where a track has been paved, frost damage is a yearly problem, dislodging or loosening slabs which then harbour water and dynamic deterioration sets in. Ride as lightly as you can, respect the surface and beware of loose stones that could unseat you.

Winter weather

There are many winter days which are perfect for riding. Soft peaty trails are frozen solid, wheels crunch through thin ice and the visibility is wonderfully good due to a lack of moisture in the air. Some of the best riding days ever are to be had in the coldest months, but go well dressed and well prepared. The moors and high hills should never be underestimated in winter. The higher you climb, the more exposed you become. Never be afraid to leave the hills if conditions start to deteriorate, the sooner the better.

Snow in winter is a probability rather than a possibility in the hills in this part of the country, but it does not make off-road riding that much more difficult unless it is very deep. Snow will cling to you and possibly make route finding more difficult by disguising tracks and impairing visibility. The answer is to stick to low level or well-defined routes if there is a possibility of snow.

Forecasts

Weather forecasts vary considerably in accuracy, often the local forecast is very different to the national prediction, but the local forecasters should know best for their own area. Meteorologists now admit that one in five forecasts is wrong, so you have an 80 per cent chance of it being correct. Get as good a forecast as you can as close to your time of departure as possible. Telephone or fax forecasts are usually updated around 6 am and provide the most up-to-date service available to the general public.

Mature trees on the Glen Road, Glentress

Family cycling

Traffic-free cycling on good surfaces is the key to enjoyable family cycling. The easy and some of the medium rides in Chapter 3 are suitable for families. Below are further details on family-friendly cycling in Central Scotland.

The Cowal peninsula from the Gourock ferry

Converted railways

By far the best family cycling routes, converted railway paths are traffic free, devoid of steep hills and usually well drained. There is much to see and learn on the railway routes: the hedgerows always have been havens for wildlife, even when the railways were operational. And, of course, there is the magnificent architecture.

Forests

A great facility for family riding are the forestry areas. They are tougher than the railways because most forests have been established in hill country where it is considered the best use of the land, but the extra effort is well worthwhile, getting you out into the depths of the countryside, usually on waymarked trails into a totally new environment. Once you become familiar with the ways of the forests, you can devise your own routes of a severity to suit your ability and your mood, perhaps venturing into woods where there are no waymarked routes, relying on your own powers of navigation. This is a most satisfying way to go mountain biking.

Another attraction of forests is the possibility of all-year riding. Even when there is snow on the ground, the low-level rides will have been traversed by forestry vehicles in the normal course of their business, compressing the snow into a rideable surface. If you run out of traction on the heights during a Cowal peninsula ride, escape to the valley is never far away. The views you get from open corners and elevated roads are great at any time of year, but even better in the winter, and you will probably be the only person there.

The Queen Elizabeth Forest Park embraces both the Highlands and the Lowlands with woodlands as far apart as the eastern shores of Loch Lomond and Strathyre, to the north of Callander. The bulk of the forestry is centred around Aberfoyle and crosses the actual Highland Boundary Fault, the geological separation of the Highlands from the Lowlands. Achray Forest is most definitely Highland, steep and rocky, while the great forest of Loch Ard, which embraces the headwaters of the River Forth, is more gentle, although in this part of the world it is only a matter of degree! There are several waymarked cycle routes in addition to those featured in this guide, some less taxing, others where it is possible to amalgamate and create longer tours.

The start of the Highlands at Aberfoyle

Trail techniques

Forests

Forests may appear to be wild and remote places, but they are in fact a workplace and an industrial environment. Respect any warning signs and keep well clear of any ongoing forestry work. If you encounter timber operations stop until you are waved through. This applies especially to vehicles loading timber and tree felling. Expect the unexpected, you may encounter a huge logging lorry around any corner, graders repairing the roads, deer, pedestrians, or other bikers, so keep your speed down and ride so that you can always pull up within the distance you can see clearly in front of you.

On the Bermuda Triangle ride

Waymarked routes within forests are not permanent features, although most of them remain unaltered for many years. They may be closed or diverted because of harvesting, motor sport events or wind damage, but the local foresters always try to post details either at the main forest entrance or at the start of the rides. In the case of the Queen Elizabeth Forest Park (see page 23) information is always posted at David Marshall Lodge, Aberfoyle. If you arrive at the forest to find the ride has been altered, or even that it does not exist any more, modify your plans accordingly. There will be another route within a reasonable distance and you can try again at a later date.

Farm roads and stony byways

Large agricultural vehicles are totally unaffected by loose stones, ruts and water, unlike cyclists and mountain bikers. The answer is to ride firmly but not too fast and at the same time not slow enough that your course will be deflected by loose stones and undulations. Try to assess the depth of water in large ruts, it may be surprisingly deep. You can ride along the ridge in the middle but this often becomes littered with loose stones thrown up by vehicle wheels.

Braking and steering on any loose surface is difficult. Always be on the look out for the 'marbles' on the outside of bends, broken sections surrounding puddles and stony washouts where little streams cross the track.

Rocks

There are rocks on the difficult routes on Arran in this guide. You will need to walk for several sections. Ensure you have got the bike well balanced when carrying it, watch where you put your feet, especially at the height of summer when the coastal vegetation can be dense, but at the same time respect the environment by causing as little disturbance as possible.

The sun promising to make an appearance across Lock Eck with Beinn Bheag in the middle distance

Chapter 2: Setting up, setting out and coming home

The Mountain Bike

Mountain Bikes (MTBs) are one of the most common types of bike in use today. Their main attraction is their versatility: they can be used for commuting, gentle family outings, exhilarating technical challenges and expeditions. They cost anything from £150– £3,000. The rides in this guide are suitable for an 'everyday' mountain bike.

1 Tough frames made from high tensile steel tubing – cromoly tubing is good because it is very strong, relatively light and inexpensive.

2 Saddle – there are two types, shown here is a micro-adjusting saddle for finer position adjustment. The clip type is also commonly used. Most saddles are designed for men and can be extremely uncomfortable on the female form. Women are advised to invest in a saddle designed for them.

3 Wide alloy rims are better than steel, they are easier to straighten, lighter, and provide better braking performance in the wet.

4 There are many types of tyres for MTBs – fat tyres with deep treads are good for mixed on and off-road cycling; thinner, shallow tread tyres are better for road riding.

5 Flat handlebars for an upright riding position.

6 Bar ends provide an extra hand position, useful for easier climbing and cruising on the flat.

7 Derailleur gears – fitted on all MTBs and provide 10-24 gears. The average MTB has 15-18 speeds which is sufficient for easy and medium grade rides. A minimum of 21 gears is necessary for tough off-road routes.

8 Gear shifters – there are four types; Shimano Rapidfire, thumb shifters, grip shifters and down type shifters for road bikes. The most common are rapidfire (shown here) and grip shifters.

9 Grips.

10 Indexed gears – mounted on the handlebar for accessible operation, the gear lever provides an audible and tactile click to indicate a gear change. Some bikes have a switch which disables the indexing.

11 Cantilever brakes – more powerful than traditional caliper brakes and essential for stopping quickly.

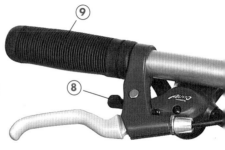

Sizing up

When buying a new or second-hand bike it is important to get one that is the correct size. Too big or too small and you could end up with numerous aches and strains. Follow the guidelines below and you should end up with a bike that is suited to your height and frame and is enjoyable to ride.

Sizing

There should be 7-10 cms (3-4 inches) between you and the cross bar when standing astride the bike – this is important if you have to jump off quickly.

Heading

SADDLE HEIGHT – adjust the saddle so that your hips don't rock when pedalling. When the ball of the foot is resting on the pedal, at the bottom of the rotation, the knee should be slightly bent.

◄ POSITION – adjust back or forward so that when the knee is flexed at 45 degrees, the knee and pedal axle are in a straight line.

ANGLE – experiment for a comfortable position.

Handlebars

Height – there is no right or wrong height, adjust for a comfortable fit.

◀ Reach – a good guide is to ensure that your back is at 45 degrees when in a natural riding position, but experiment for personal preference.

Sizing children's bikes

Kids love riding bikes. Mountain bikes are perfect because they get them off the streets and out of the way of traffic. There are many different grades of tracks that are suitable for children to ride on with their parents, a number of which are featured in Chapter 3. Good children's mountain bikes that offer the same sort of features as adult bikes are now available.

Sizing a mountain bike for a child is the same as for an adult. It may be tempting to buy a larger size so that it lasts longer but this is not a good idea because a child will have less control over the bike and may lose confidence.

Good-fitting helmets are particularly important for children (*see* pp 30-31, Essential accessories). Deck your child out with a full complement of reflectors (*see* pp 46-47, Safety and emergency).

Essential accessories

Helmet – always wear a helmet, they can limit damage to one of the most vulnerable parts of the body. A good fit is essential, they should be snug and move with the scalp if you wiggle your eyebrows but not tight enough to pinch the sides of your head. A helmet that does not fit will not offer adequate protection.

Make sure a new helmet conforms to one of the following standards: Snell, ANSI, Eu, and BSI.

If you do have an accident, take the helmet back to the shop that sold it to you for checking. Helmets are designed to withstand one crash and damage is not always apparent to the eye.

Children's helmets

A child's head is especially vulnerable. Get children, and reluctant teenagers, into the habit of wearing a helmet from the start. Remember

- don't buy a helmet for a child to grow into, a good fit is important
- make sure the helmet sits low enough on the head but has little side to side movement
- ensure the strap is adjusted so that the helmet cannot move
- avoid pinching a child's neck in the snap lock buckle, it is painful. Ask them to hold their chin up
- buy a helmet with some reflective material on the outer shell

Not essential but fun

A bike computer: they are useful for seeing how far you have gone and can tell you your maximum speed, average speed, total accumulated mileage and the time. Most have seven functions and are waterproof.

Tool kit 4, 5, and 6mm allen keys, multi tool (a selection of tools in a penknife format), small pliers, chain rivet extractor, chain ring bolt, spare chain links.

Puncture repair kit

Spare inner tube

Pump

Lights necessary even if you don't expect to be riding in the dusk or dark. You may get delayed. LED lights are compact, light and have a 3-4 month battery life.

Reflective belt in case you run out of daylight or the weather changes dramatically.

Map this guide uses Ordnance Survey Landranger 1:50,000. You are advised to buy the relevant map(s) for your route and not rely on the maps reproduced in this guide.

Compass

Oil in a small tin or grease in a packet.

Water bottle they vary in size from 0.75 litres to 1.5 litres.

Money and small change or a phone card for emergencies.

A watch to ensure you start the return journey in good time.

Bumbag for carrying money and valuables.

Panniers for carrying food and spare clothing.

Clothing for all weathers

There is a lot of specialist cycling gear in bike shops and the range can be rather daunting to an occasional or novice cyclist. Most people cannot go out and buy the complete outfit in one go and will have to make do with what is in the wardrobe with perhaps one or two specialist items. Here are some general guidelines to cope with the vagaries of the British weather and help make your ride as comfortable as possible.

- Wear loose clothing that allows complete freedom of movement.
- Choose materials such as cotton or Lycra mixes which can breathe.
- If you buy one item of cycling gear, make it a pair of padded cycling shorts, they provide comfort from the saddle and are designed not to chafe the skin.

Being properly dressed for bad weather and good (below) makes riding enjoyable

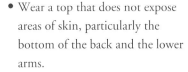

- Wear a top that does not expose areas of skin, particularly the bottom of the back and the lower arms.
- Wear, or pack, several layers of clothing so that you can shed or add as the temperature changes.
- Make sure the layer closest to your skin is made of a material that can breathe.
- Always take a waterproof; cycling in cold wet clothes is miserable.
- Use glasses to protect your eyes from dust, insects and bright sunshine. Specialist cycling glasses (above right) are designed for that purpose.
- Gloves can stop you shredding your hands if you come off the bike and padded ones provide some shock absorption.
  - It is not essential to buy cycling shoes, although if you intend to cycle very regularly it might be a good idea. Tennis shoes and trainers are good substitutes.

Fine weather essentials

- sunglasses
- sun cream
- long sleeved top in case it gets chilly

specialist glasses protect the eyes and are less likely to break

A long sleeved top for riding off-road.

Foul weather essentials

- hat
- scarf
- thermal top and bottom
- several long-sleeved tops for layering
- waterproof boots
- waterproof gloves
- A thermal layer next to the skin in wet or cold conditions maintains core warmth (chest and back)
- A balaclava keeps head and ears warm when it is cold
- Two pairs of gloves and socks keep extremities from getting icy in winter

Wash padded cycling shorts after every ride to keep them in good condition

Tips

- Legs and arms can get scratched when riding off-road, long sleeves and trousers may be more appropriate
- Keep spare clothes in the car – muddy clothes do not mix well with the insides of pubs and tearooms
- Keep a black bin liner in the car for wet and muddy clothes

padded gloves

Food and drink

Your body uses a lot of energy when cycling, particularly on tougher rides, so it is very important to carry food and drink with you, even on the shortest rides. If you rely on the pub or teashop they will inevitably be closed. And if you get delayed by a mechanical fault or an injury, it could be some time before you get to the next watering hole.

The golden rules are to eat before you are hungry and drink before you are thirsty. It is a good idea to find some shelter when you stop for refreshment to avoid getting chilled, particularly in exposed areas of the country. A hollow in the ground will do.

Please remember to take all litter with you when you have finished your snack. Litter can be a major hazard to wildlife and spoils the countryside for other people.

Flapjacks are a favourite mountain biker's snack

Remember to eat before you are hungry

Food

Snacking is better than having one big meal. Complex carbohydrates are the best energy givers. They take longer to digest and release their nutrients at a steady rate. Chocolate and sweet snacks give an immediate energy boost which fades rapidly. Flapjacks, malt loaf, dried fruit, nuts and bananas are all nutritious and easy to carry. Specialist cycling food is sometimes overhyped and overpriced but may be worth a try.

Complex carbohydrates such as bananas, dried fruit and nuts provide energy while you are on the trail

Drink

Water is by far the best drink to carry with you because it is easily absorbed by the body. Dehydration can happen quickly, particularly on long rides in hot weather, therefore aim to drink every 20-30 minutes. Don't underestimate how much water your body can lose on a hard trip, even in winter. Carry some extra water in the car. Don't drink from a stream unless you are sure it is close to a good spring. Avoid sweet and fizzy drinks.

Tip

Clear water bottles help you see if the bottle has gone mouldy and tell you how much is in there.

Preparing your bike

Before you start out on a journey it is good to get into the habit of a pre-ride check. If you are not confident about doing it yourself, many shops will oblige for a small fee. However, the steps below are fairly easy to accomplish and give you the best chance of a trouble-free ride.

1 ► Ensure that all the bolts on the bike are tight.

2 Run through the gears and ensure that the changes are crisp.

3 Look for damaged or stiff links in the chain: spinning the cranks backwards should show you if there is a problem because the chain will jump.

4 Check there is enough lubrication on the chain.

5 Pull on the brake lever, if it moves easily a long way towards the handlebar, the brakes need adjusting.

6 Worn brake blocks will not do their job. Replace them when it becomes necessary.

7 All the strands on a cable should be twisted together. Frayed or rusty brake cable must be replaced immediately.

8 Inspect tyres for flints and thorns, gouges from brake blocks and general wear. Worn or damaged tyres are more prone to puncture.

9 Measure the tyre pressure with a pressure gauge. You will find the recommended pressure marked on the sides of the tyre.

If you don't have a gauge, squeeze the tyre sides: you should be able to push your thumb about a ½ cm (¼ inch) into a correctly inflated mountain bike tyre.

Ensure tyres are well inflated for off-road surfaces where punctures are more likely.

10 ▶ Spin the wheels to check if they are straight, using the brake blocks as a guide. Listen for scuffing noises which indicate a dent. Small dents can be hammered out with a rubber mallet, larger ones mean the wheels need replacing.

11 Look for bent and damaged spokes.

Transporting your bike

A lot of people live in cities and cities tend to be a long way from areas where people want to ride their mountain bikes. It is possible to get to the start of some of the routes in this book by train. However, the most usual method of transporting your bike is on, in or behind the car.

By car

Roof racks, boot racks and tow bar racks are the alternatives to bagging (see box) when transporting your bike by car, although just removing the wheels and saddle may be enough to fit a small bike or bikes into a large car. Secure fixing and regular checking is of the utmost importance whichever of the options you choose.

Tow bar racks are secure and won't damage the car's paint work.

Be legal

Boot and tow bar racks cover up your rear tail lights and number plate. You must use a tow plate with your number plate attached so that other road users can clearly see your brakes and number plate. Many police forces are vigilant about this and may take action if you are in breach of the law.

Bagging your bike

Dismantling your bike and carrying it in a bag is a good way of getting round reluctant train and coach operators and also transporting your bike inside your car. It is important to pad the tubing and wheel to prevent scratches and knocks. It is also essential to double check that you have put all the components into the bag along with the tools needed for reassembly at your destination.

Boot and roof racks

Boot racks are becoming one of the most popular ways of transporting bikes. Up to 99 per cent of cars can be fitted with a boot rack: they are easy to attach and relatively cheap. Most are designed to carry up to three bikes. Roof rack manufacturers offer fitting kits to allow you to carry anything from skis to canoes, including bikes. They can be carried upside down, upright and with the front wheel removed. See the box opposite to ensure you are travelling legally.

Tow bar racks

These can save damage to the body work of your car and are as strong and secure as a boot rack.

By train

Most rail networks will let you take your bike onto their trains. However, policy varies from region to region and country to country so always check before arriving at the station.

By coach and bus

Coach and bus companies have their own policies on transporting bikes, so check in advance that you will be allowed on.

By air

Most major airlines will carry your bike. Check with the airline when you book your tickets. Your bike will have to be boxed up or bagged (*see* above).

Preparing yourself: stretching

Cycling is good exercise and an excellent way of keeping in shape. Like all forms of exercise, you are far less likely to get an injury if you make sure your muscles are warmed up before you start. Simple stretches will greatly improve your flexibility and endurance. The following steps should take 5-10 minutes.

Back

Sit on the floor with your legs stretched out in front of you. Bend your body forwards from the waist/hip aiming to put your nose on your knees. It doesn't matter if you can bend just a couple of inches or all the way. Stop as soon as it hurts.

Legs

Your legs are going to work hardest of all, particularly on a long ride with several climbs. These three exercises will prepare you for what is to come.

◄ Stretch the calf muscles by extending one leg straight behind you, foot flat on the floor, and holding the stretch for 30 seconds. Move your rear foot further back and hold this for 30 seconds. Repeat with the other leg.

Shenuller

Clasp your hands
together behind you by
reaching your left hand
over your shoulder so
that your right elbow is
pointing straight up and
your left hand up behind
the back. Hold the
position for 30 seconds.
Repeat, reversing the
position of the arms.

Neck

Stand relaxed and turn your
head from left to right
slowly, holding it for at
least 30 seconds at the
farthest reach each side.
Then gently raise and
lower your chin.

Groin

Sit on the floor with your
legs apart at 45 degrees or
as far as they will go. With
both hands, reach towards
the right foot and hold the
position for 30 seconds.
Repeat to the left.

◀ Stand on one leg and bring the knee of your
other leg up towards your chin. Clasp your hands
together around the raised leg and pull it up to
your chest, keeping your back straight.
Hold the position for 30 seconds.
Repeat with the other leg.

▶ To stretch the hamstring,
cross one leg in front of the
other, keeping your feet
close together. Gently bend
forwards as far as you can go from the
waist/hip, keeping your back straight.
Hold this position for 30 seconds.
Repeat, crossing the other leg in front.

41

On the trail

When out riding, remember that there are other people using the trails for their own enjoyment. Polite, helpful and considerate conduct is important so that mountain bikers are not seen as a menace by the rest of the population. Following the MTB code below will make you a good ambassador for all mountain bikers.

MTB code

1 Give way to other trail users.
2 Always be courteous to other trail users.
3 Take every bit of rubbish away with you.
4 Leave gates as you find them.
5 Never skid, especially on wet soft ground (to avoid erosion).
6 Ride with respect for your surroundings.
7 Check that you have legal access to the land you are on.
8 Always take note of MOD flagpoles.
9 Warn horses and walkers of your approach by ringing your bell, singing, whistling or talking to your cycle partners.

Courtesy to other trail users costs nothing and enhances the reputation of mountain biking

Below are a few tips to make your life easier and safer out on the trail.

- Plan your ride with the weakest member of your group in mind.
- Let the slowest rider set the pace.
- Off-road, leave a reasonable distance between you and the rider in front.
- The deepest part of a puddle is where vehicle wheels go; try the middle higher ground.
- Anticipate hills; change to the right gear in good time.
- On-road, help weaker riders by getting them to ride in your slipstream.
- Remove vegetation from derailleurs (gears) immediately to prevent against damage.
- Faster riders should go ahead and open and close gates for the rest of the group to balance the differences in strength.
- Keep money and keys with you at all times, even if you leave other gear on the bike.
- Fold your map to the section you need in the dry and out of the wind.

Mountain bikers have to share many trails with other users

Navigation

It is easy to get lost while mountain biking. A combination of tight twisty trails and changing scenery makes it easy to become disorientated and lose your sense of direction. Routes also look different according to the time of year.

A LWAYS CARRY a map of the area. You will find the number and name of the map for each ride in this guide in the ride specification box. Observation is the key to successful navigation in unknown territory. Make a mental note of distinctive features such as steep contours, rivers, forested areas and tracks before you begin and look for them on route.

If you become lost, stay in a group and work together to find your way home. Don't separate; both parties may end up lost! Retrace your steps to a point where you know where you are. If necessary go back to the start the way you came. Try to rejoin the route at a later stage or find a road alternative on the map. If you can't do this, stop at the next signpost or landmark, consult your map and take a compass bearing.

Checking the map to decide in which direction to continue

Taking a compass bearing

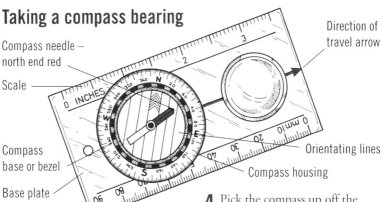

Compass needle – north end red

Scale

Compass base or bezel

Base plate

Direction of travel arrow

Orientating lines

Compass housing

A compass becomes essential once you are lost and is always useful in forestry areas. The illustration above shows the most useful type of compass which usually comes with instructions. The following steps will help you determine in which direction to travel according to the route on your map.

1 Roughly orientate the map so the north edge is facing north.

2 Place the compass flat on the map with the long edge of the baseplate along the desired direction of travel. In other words either connecting, or in line with, where you are currently standing and the next point on the route.

3 Rotate the capsule until the N on the compass dial or bezel, not the needle, points to North on the map. You have now taken a bearing.

4 Pick the compass up off the map and turn yourself around until the red end of the needle points to N on the compass dial and lines up with the orientating lines in the base of the dial. The large 'direction of travel' arrow will now point precisely at your destination.

5 Choose a landmark on this line of travel and ride towards it without looking at the compass: there is no need and minor curves and deviations in the track will only confuse the issue.

6 When you reach this first landmark repeat the procedure until you reach your destination.

Safety and emergency

Safety is, of course, a priority – particularly if you are riding with children. There is a lot that common sense will tell you. However, a few reminders are always useful.

Safety precautions

- Always wear a helmet, even on the shortest route. You can never predict what other track and road users are going to do. The one time you go out without your helmet on is the time you will most need it. Nothing can prevent the damage that a car speeding at 60mph causes, but protecting your head can limit injury in lot of instances.

- Take great care crossing roads, particularly main A roads. Dismount, and use a pedestrian crossing if there is one. Read ahead in the ride directions to alert yourself to road crossings and warn others in your group, especially children, that a road is coming up.

- Avoid riding on busy roads with young children and inexperienced riders. Try to find a quieter alternative.

- If you are riding in poor light or at night, make sure your lights are on and that you are wearing some reflective clothing. Ankle bands are particularly good at alerting car drivers to your presence. Also, kit your children out with the full range of reflectors.

- Check the local weather forecast before you embark on a ride, particularly if you intend to be out for a long time. Try to make a educated guess as to whether it is riding weather.

- Tell someone where you are going and, if possible, leave a marked up map of the area at home. It will help locate you in the event of a rescue team being called out.

- Take adequate supplies of food and drink to prevent against dehydration. Don't be over ambitious. Choose a ride well within your capabilities or you might find yourself in trouble in the middle of a route.

What to do in emergencies

Due to the nature of off-road riding it is quite possible that you may have to deal with an accident involving another rider. There are several things to remember:

- Place the rider in the recovery position using the minimum of movement (see First aid pp48-49). Keep the rider warm and place a jacket underneath their head for comfort
- If they have sustained a head injury do not remove their helmet unless they are bleeding severely
- Do not give food in case they need to be operated on in a hurry
- If you have to leave an injured rider to seek assistance make sure that they are warm and feel able to stay awake
- Make a note of where you have left them on your map and mark the spot with a piece of bright clothing held down by a stone or attached to a tree
- Get help as quickly as possible

Keep an accident victim warm and get help as soon as possible

First Aid

Every mountain biker, indeed every cyclist, comes off their bike sooner or later. It is a good idea to carry a small first aid kit with you on trips to cope with cut and bruises.

When a person is seriously injured the priority is to ring 999 and get an ambulance to them as quickly as possible. Describe your location as accurately as you can. It is useful to be able to tell the emergency services as much as possible about the accident and the state of the patient when they arrive.

Minor injuries

• Small cuts and grazes can be rinsed with cold water from a drinking bottle. Apply some antiseptic and cover with a clean plaster.

• Dizziness and faintness might occur after a crash or spill. Sit down comfortably until the feeling passes. If it doesn't improve place the head between the knees.

Simple first aid kit

• As a minimum, take the following: water bottle, antiseptic lotion or cream, plasters, cottonwool.

Major injuries

• If someone has a serious crash or spill remaining calm is vital. You cannot help another person if you are in a panic. Don't expect too much of yourself: you may be suffering from shock as well as the injured party.

• Assess the situation. Stop the traffic if it may be a danger to the injured person and try to enlist the help of a third party.

- Assess the injured. Are they conscious? If they are, ask them how they feel and if they can describe their injuries.

- Bleeding needs to be stopped. If possible raise the wound and apply a compress firmly over the bleeding area until it ceases.

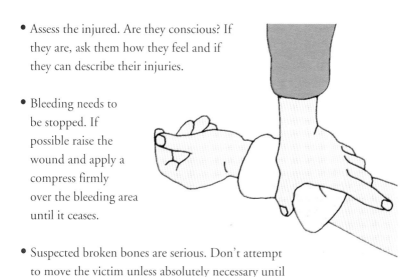

- Suspected broken bones are serious. Don't attempt to move the victim unless absolutely necessary until professional help arrives.

- Check for a pulse by placing your fingers on the victim's voice box. If there is no pulse and their breathing has stopped you could try resuscitation – however, only do so if you know how.

- Keep the injured person warm, offer reassuring words and hold their hand until help arrives. Don't give them food or drink in case they need an emergency operation.

- If you are sure the injured person does not have a spinal injury, place them in the recovery position.

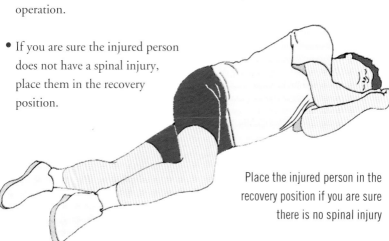

Place the injured person in the recovery position if you are sure there is no spinal injury

When you get home

Cleaning the bike after a ride is a job most people hate and would skip if they had any choice. However, it is essential if you want to maximise the life of your bike and ensure it is always in good working order. The following is a six step procedure which should take about 10 minutes.

Tools

Ideally use a hose with a brush head and soap reservoir, car shampoo and WD40 for lubrication. Keep high pressure water spraying away from the bearings in case the seals cannot withstand a strong jet of water.

1 Hose off the worst of the mud while it is still wet.

2 Use a hose brush head (or a brush and hose) to scrub off any lumps of mud and finish the initial rinse.

3 Using car shampoo, gently scrub off remaining dirt with soapy water.

4 Rinse off the soap with plain water and repeat the shampoo and rinse if necessary.

5 Use degreaser on ground-in dirt and rinse off with plain water.

6 Let the water drip off and spray exposed metal or moving parts with WD40.

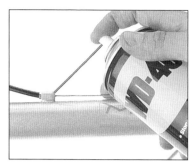

Lubrication

WD40 is an adequate and relatively cheap oil for general lubrication. Apply it immediately after cleaning to:

1 rear brake pivots
2 rear mech pivot points
3 rear mech jockey wheels
4 front mech points

5 brake lever pivots
6 front brake pivots
7 cable ends at the stops

Use a heavier oil such as standard mineral-based medium weight oil for the chain.

Chapter 3: The rides

1 Longniddry to Haddington

This is a quiet, easy ride through beautiful farmland starting in the ancient village of Longniddry, which is now a commuter town for Edinburgh but was once inhabited by weavers and agricultural workers. The ride runs to Haddington, the fine county town of East Lothian.

GRADE	easy
DISTANCE	17.6 kms (10.9 miles)
TIME	allow 2 hours
MAP	OS Landranger 66 Edinburgh and Midlothian area
GRID REF AT START	446762
PARKING	80 spaces at Longniddry railway station
TERRAIN	dedicated railway path, quiet roads, last 400 m (365 yds) can be busy.
TRAINS	nearest station, Longniddry. Regular commuter services
SEASONAL SUITABILITY	all year
SURFACE	dressed railway trackbed, well drained, mostly smooth
CLIMBS/DESCENTS	n/a
REFRESHMENTS	Victoria Inn and Plough Inn, Haddington; Longniddry Inn opposite the railway station

1 Wheel your bike on to the platform of Longniddry railway station, carry it across the metal footbridge, then exit on to the old railway path via a stout galvanised gate. Turn left and ride east very close to the railway.

2 0.3 kms (0.2 miles) further on is the official start to the railway path and a signpost for Haddington 7.25 kms (4.5 miles). Go straight on beyond the five-bar gate. Cross a small wooden bridge over a farm road and look for views of the vast Firth of Forth. Redhouse is visible across the fields to the left. Head south-west into the countryside. Continue for 4.6 kms (2.8 miles).

3 Go straight on at Merryhatton bridge for 1.6 kms (1 mile).

4 Go straight on under the 1995 A1 Great North Road.

5 After 0.4 kms (0.3 miles) use the pelican cycle crossing to go straight across, although you will encounter little traffic.

6 The end of the railway path is 0.3 kms (0.2 miles) further on. Do not ride on into the rubbish under the bridge. Instead turn right at the T-junction on to a public road *over* the bridge.

© Crown Copyright

7 At the T-junction with West Road in Haddington turn left. Continue for 0.9 kms (0.6 miles).

8 Go straight on at the crossroad with traffic lights signposted 'Town Centre'.

9 The outward leg ends at Town House, Haddington town centre. Stop for refreshment or turn around and head back.

10 Go back over the crossroad signposted 'Edinburgh and the North'.

11 After 0.9 kms (0.6 miles) turn right at a blue cycle path signpost for 'Longniddry'. A short uphill.

12 After 0.3 kms (0.2 miles) turn left on to the cycle path immediately beyond the bridge following another blue cycle path signpost for 'Longniddry'.

13 Go back over the pelican crossing, a wooden signboard says 'Longniddry'.

14 Go back under the A1 and retrace your route along the old railway to Longniddry station.

2 Lochwinnoch

For an area usually associated with industry, this ride may come as a pleasant surprise. Parts of Castle Semple Loch form a nature reserve and the route takes you above the tranquil waters of Barr Loch to Kilbirnie. It is not unusual to see wildfowl in flight or fish making huge rise rings on the surface of the lochs, a far cry from the area's recent industrial past.

GRADE easy	
DISTANCE 14.3 kms (8.9 miles)	
TIME allow 2 hours	
MAP OS Landranger 63 Firth of Clyde area	
GRID REF AT START 358591	
PARKING 100 spaces at Clyde Muirshiel Regional park, Lochwinnoch	
TERRAIN old railway track through Glengarnock, in the Cunninghame hills	
SEASONAL SUITABILITY all year	
SURFACE dressed railway trackbed, smooth throughout	
CLIMBS/DESCENTS n/a	
REFRESHMENTS none on route; shops and pubs in Lochwinnoch and Kilbirnie	

1 Start at the Clyde Muirshiel Regional Park and ride south-west along Lochlip Road. There is a blue cycleway signpost to 'Irvine' a short distance from the park entrance.

2 At Church Street continue straight on along Lochlip Road.

3 After 0.1 kms (0.1 miles) turn right into the Sports Ground following the 'Irvine' cycleway sign. Keep left of

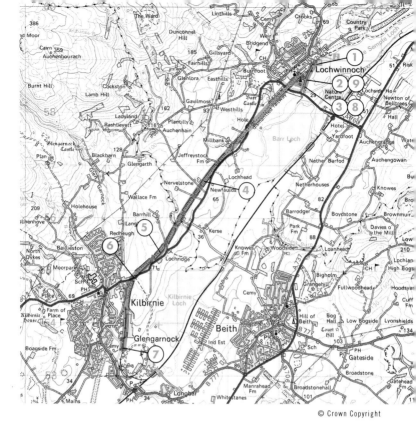

© Crown Copyright

the changing facilities and aim for the elevated railway at the far side of the football pitches. Once on the railway continue for 2.8 kms (1.8 miles).

4 Go straight on under an iron aqueduct and continue for 1.7 kms (1.1 miles).

5 Continue straight on at the second wooden aqueduct. The deep cutting carries on for some distance.

The Castle Semple Centre at Clyde Muirshiel Regional Park, Lochwinnoch

6 At Kilbirnie Bridge go straight on, on to tarmac and continue for 1.5 kms (0.9 miles). There is a path through a cutting on the right into the town if you need refreshment.

7 On reaching Kilbirnie sports fields, turn around and head back. Retrace your route along the old railway past the iron and wooden aqueducts.

8 To get back onto Lochlip Road turn left at the T-junction.

9 Go straight on past Church Street and retrace to Lochside carpark and then back to Clyde Muirshiel Regional Park.

3 Bridge of Weir

There is no better way to admire the district of Renfrewshire than from the old railway line between Johnstone and Greenock. It has been graded and well-surfaced by Sustrans who own the track. Kilmacolm, through which the route passes, has many large fine houses one of which, Windyhills, was built by Scotland's most famous architect Charles Rennie Mackintosh.

GRADE	easy
DISTANCE	11.2 kms (7.2 miles)
TIME	allow 1 hour
MAP	OS Landranger 63 Firth of Clyde area
GRID REF AT START	390655
PARKING	100 spaces behind the Gryffe Inn, Bridge of Weir
TERRAIN	flat
SEASONAL SUITABILITY	all year
SURFACE	smoothed and dressed railway trackbed, tarmac near Kilmacolm
CLIMBS/DESCENTS	n/a
REFRESHMENTS	pubs and restaurants, Bridge of Weir; the Pullman PH facilities for children, at the turning point in Kilmacolm

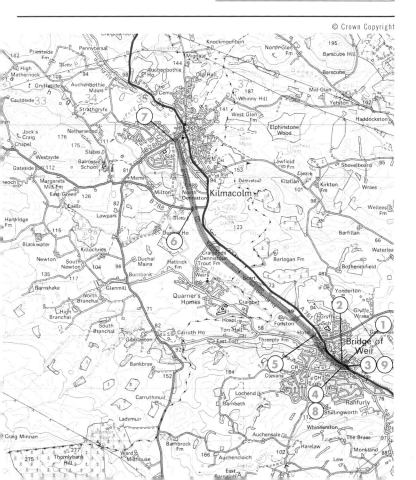

The River Gryfe and Strathgryfe from the Bridge of Weir viaduct

1 Leave the Gryffe Inn carpark and return to the A761.

2 Turn left at the T-junction with the A761. If you have very young riders in the party, walk along to the zebra crossing and then turn right into Station Road.

3 Turn right into Station Road, then left at the black posts. A blue cycleway sign says 'Kilmacolm'.

4 At the railway path, turn right across the bridges over the River Gryffe, not signposted. You are soon into open countryside.

5 After 0.8 kms (0.5 miles) at Bridge 21, go straight on for 3.1 kms (1.9 miles).

6 Go straight on over the B788 for 1.4 kms (0.9 miles) on to the tarmac section around Kilmacolm, then through the magnificent cutting to the end of this section of line.

7 At Bridge 31 there is the Pullman PH. Turn around here and head back. Retrace your route to the Bridge of Weir.

8 At the Bridge of Weir turn left off the railway path and down into the town centre.

9 Turn left at the T-junction with the A761, then right into the carpark.

4 Callander to Strathyre

A trip of almost 30 kms (19 miles) may seem long for the easy category but the old railway from Callander to Strathyre is mainly flat and, like many pleasure riders, you can confine yourself to the picturesque 7 kms (4.5 miles) stretch around Loch Lubnaig if you choose. The old line is dominated by quiet agriculture, dense woodland and the huge bulk of Ben Ledi, 879 m (2884 ft) high. On the far side of the loch, Ben Vorlich rises to a massive 984 m (3228 ft), providing some wonderful vistas on the return leg. There is a lot to see at close quarters, too. Callander is a bustling tourist town, lying on one of the main routes to the western Highlands and is in stark contrast to the peace and tranquility of this ride.

1 Start at the west end of Callander on what was the railway bridge. An old signal gantry is hidden in the trees, go down into dense woodland signposted 'Strathyre, Balquhidder. Alternative route for cyclists' for 1.4 kms (0.9 miles). The path crosses a steel bridge over the Garbh Uisge (Rough Water) and a couple of smaller wooden bridges over lesser watercourses as you ride along an elevated way through the water meadows.

GRADE easy

DISTANCE 29.6 kms (18.4 miles)

TIME allow 3 hours

MAP OS Landranger 57 Stirling and The Trossachs

GRID REF AT START 622080

PARKING ample parking near the riverside in Callander.

TERRAIN a mainly flat route amid the spectacular countryside of Strathyre

TRAINS nearest station, Dunblane

SEASONAL SUITABILITY all year,

SURFACE converted railway track, woodland path, a little forest road

CLIMBS/DESCENTS 1 gentle, 1 short steep climb/1 steep descent

REFRESHMENTS none on route; pub food in Strathyre.

2 Go straight on across Bochastle Farm access road over a couple of bike-sized cattle grids.

3 At Kilmahog go straight across the A821 taking care. You will probably need to dismount to negotiate the barrier at the far side. Continue for 2.7 kms (1.7 miles) past the Falls of Leny.

4 Go straight on at the carpark, marked on the map. Beware of traffic as you pass the bridge from the main road. Continue for 5.1 kms (3.2 miles). The access road to the forestry cabins is asphalt but beyond the chain barrier the track reverts to railway trackbed. Eventually it rises

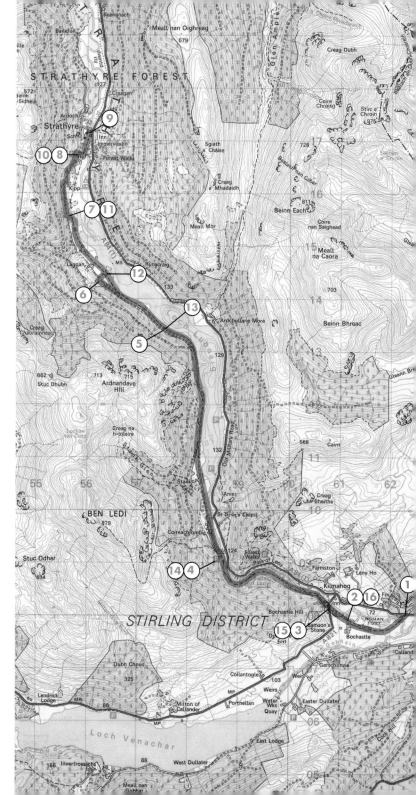

with the forest road to coincide with one of the waymarked forest tracks.

5 At the forest road junction the track merges with a road from the left. Go straight on up a gradual climb for 1.6 kms (1 mile).

6 Fork right on to a single track to rejoin the old railway signposted 'Cycleway to Strathyre'. The route is now a field away from the side of Loch Lubnaig. Pass Laggan Farm. Eventually you leave the trackbed again and climb steep hairpin bends to join the forest access road. Most people will have to walk.

7 After 1.3 kms (0.8 miles) turn right at the T-junction after a tiny cattle grid on to a good non-tarmac road. This becomes asphalt as you descend. Look for the cycleway signs at the wooden forestry houses.

8 After 1.7 kms (1.1 miles) at Strathyre forestry cottages, turn right signposted 'Cycleway to Strathyre'. Follow the signs, weaving around to a military style suspension bridge, then snake through the trees to Strathyre.

9 Refreshment is available at The Inn and the Ben Sheann Hotel in Strathyre. Turn round here and start retracing your route.

10 At the forestry cottages T-junction, turn left up the hill. This time the tarmac will give way to hard-packed dirt as you climb.

11 After 1.7 kms (1.1 miles) turn left over the tiny cattle grid at the top of the hairpins, signposted 'Cycleway to Callander' and also with red and green forestry waymarkers. Take care down the hairpins then follow the old railway for 1.3 kms (0.8 miles).

12 Go straight on on the grassy railway by the lochside: this is where the return journey differs from the outbound route, although it may be advisable to retrace up and over the higher forest track in wet weather.

13 After 1.6 kms (1 mile) go straight on as the track merges with a forest road coming down the hill on your right. Continue for 5 kms (3.1 miles).

14 Go straight on at the carpark. Continue for 2.7 kms (1.7 miles).

15 Cross the A821 taking care to watch for traffic.

16 Go back across the bike size grids, straight on over the farm approach road towards Callander to the finish 1.4 kms (0.9 miles) ahead.

5 Smokin' Arbroath

Arbroath is famous for its smokies, smoke-cured haddock which can be eaten hot or cold. It also holds a special place in Scottish history because Arbroath Abbey was where Scotland's nobles swore their independence from England in 1320. The outward leg of the route uses an old railway line running through a valley or cuttings but you return through rich farmland known for potatoes and soft fruits.

GRADE	easy
DISTANCE	8.4 kms (5.2 miles)
TIME	allow 1.5 hours
MAP	OS Landranger 54 Dundee to Montrose
GRID REF AT START	639429
PARKING	8 spaces in St Vigean's carpark next to parish hall
TERRAIN	rolling Angus countryside
TRAINS	nearest station Arbroath
SEASONAL SUITABILITY	all year
SURFACE	compact well-drained railway trackbed and quiet country roads
CLIMBS/DESCENTS	1 short, gentle climb/ 1 descent to finish
REFRESHMENTS	none on route; full facilities, Arbroath

1 Set off north-west through St Vigean's churchyard extension across the road from the church on the mound, turning right across a small wooden bridge within 50 m (55 yds). Once you have negotiated the barriers, follow the burn (stream) upstream past sizable trees, boggy meadows and well-used pasture.

2 After 1 km (0.6 miles) go straight across the road at the end of the bridge. The view of the road is not good but you will hear any vehicles coming down the hill – the bends at the bridge are so tight that a very slow approach is inevitable. The path is narrowed by vegetation.

3 At a carpark go straight on. Stick with the railway, do not use the private road to Kyleakin Villa. There are a number of barriers to negotiate. Lift the bike over the gates if necessary.

4 Go straight on at the crossroad at Kyleakin Villa. The golf course and some new houses are to the right, agricultural heartland to the left. Continue for 2.5 kms (1.6 miles). Look out for the old platform at Letham Grange just before the end of the line.

5 At the end of railway path turn left at the T-junction, not signposted. Ride gently uphill with fine beech trees into more open country for 0.2 kms (0.1 miles).

6 At the end of the Peebles road turn left signposted 'Peebles, Mains of Letham'. Continue for 2.8 kms

(1.8 miles) along a pleasant undulating road through fields.

7 Go straight on past East and West Cottages, along the side of the airfield for 0.8 kms (0.5 miles).

8 At the T-junction with the main road, turn left, then left again immediately, signposted 'St Vigean's' continue for 0.6 kms (0.4 miles) to the finish. This is a new road on the northern fringe of Arbroath, but you can take a short cut on the old road. Take care past Brae Heid where the hill can come as a bit of a surprise.

6 Inverkeilor and the Lunan Water

This ride is an ideal launch pad for new riders. Using mainly quiet lanes, the route takes you through rolling Angus countryside, home of the most famous beef breed in the world, the Aberdeen Angus. The area is intensively farmed and the result is an ordered appearance. But the sea and the great mountains of the Grampians are not far away, providing a reminder that this area encompasses all the landscapes of Scotland.

GRADE medium	
DISTANCE 18.6 kms (11.6 miles)	
TIME allow 1.5 hours	
MAP OS Landranger 54 Dundee to Montrose	
GRID REF AT START 664496	
PARKING 2 spaces at the sewerage filter site next to the Inverkeilor kirk, or with care on the village street	
TERRAIN rolling rural countryside	
TRAINS nearest stations, Arbroath, Montrose	
SEASONAL SUITABILITY all year	
SURFACE mainly tarmac	
CLIMBS/DESCENTS 4 short steep climbs on tarmac/1 short steep descent, several gentler downhills, 1 good off-road descent	
REFRESHMENTS none on route; Chance Inn, Inverkeilor	

1 Depart west from the kirk to the A92.

2 Take care at the junction with the A92 which is an offset crossroad, turn right then immediately left on to the B965 signposted 'Letham Grange'.

3 After 0.6 kms (0.4 miles) turn right downhill into a narrow road, no signpost but '3T' weight limit.

4 Cross over the bridge then turn left at the T-junction uphill. This is very narrow.

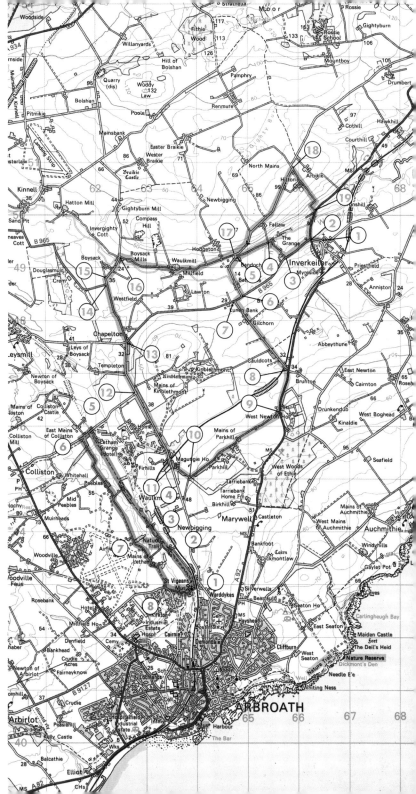

5 At Bandoch turn left at the strange shaped crossroad. Remember this junction. Continue for 0.9 kms (0.6 miles).

6 Turn right at the T-junction with the B965, no signpost.

7 Shortly, turn left signposted 'Cauldcots. Arbroath avoiding low bridge'. Continue for 1.7 kms (1.1 miles).

8 After Cauldcots turn right at the T-junction with the A92, signposted 'Arbroath'. Take care. Continue for 0.9 kms (0.5 miles).

9 At West Newton House turn right signposted 'Letham Grange'. Continue for 2.1 kms (1.3 miles).

10 Turn right into a very narrow road, with white lines at the junction, no signpost.

11 At Magungie House turn right at the T-junction, no signpost. This unclassified road is wider and grander than the B965. Continue for 1.6 kms (1 mile).

12 Go straight on past a road on the left, towards 'Friockheim'. Do not go to Letham Grange. Continue for 1 km (0.6 miles).

Hilton, near Inverkeilor. You can just see Lunan Bay in the distance

13 At the crossroad in Chapelton, go straight on signposted 'B965 Friockheim'. Continue for 1.1 kms (0.7 miles).

14 Go straight ahead, leaving the B965, on to an unclassified road signposted 'Boysack'.

15 Very shortly fork right with 'main' road. No signpost.

16 At Boysack Mill go over the bridge then turn right. Continue for 2.5 kms (1.5 miles). This very narrow road is sometimes used by large wagons from the quarry, vehicles from the garage at Hodgeton, and some agricultural traffic.

17 At the same junction as direction no.5, take the high road, straight on up the hill. Continue for 2.1 kms (1.3 miles).

18 Turn right at Hilton into the farm road, then keep left down the grass track on the north east side of the farm.

19 Turn right at the T-junction with the A92. Take care. Continue for 0.6 kms (0.4 miles) and turn left at the signpost for 'Inverkeilor' back to the start.

7 The Bermuda Triangle

The unspectacular rolling nature of the Lammermuir Hills hides many treasures, not least the sparkling burns, many of which provide water for the surrounding district. At direction number 10 the standing stone near the wall commemorates the 12th Earl of Lauderdale who was killed by lightning here whilst shooting grouse. Please treat the well-managed moorland with common sense and consideration.

GRADE	medium
DISTANCE	28 kms (17.4 miles)
TIME	allow 2.75 hours
MAP	OS Landranger 73 Peebles, Galashiels and surrounding area
GRID REF AT START	531475
PARKING	10 spaces outside Lauder Town Hall
TERRAIN	rolling Lauderdale hills
SEASONAL SUITABILITY	all year (but see page 17 for details of nesting and shooting seasons)
SURFACE	tarmac, good grouse roads, a stretch of moorland track which varies from a well-defined 4-wheel-drive twin track to a sheep trod in width
CLIMBS/DESCENTS	2 short and steep, 2 longer gentler climbs/several off-road descents, 1 steep tarmac descent
REFRESHMENTS	none on route

1 From Lauder Town Hall go north-west on the A68 for 0.5 kms (0.3 miles).

2 At Lauder War Memorial go straight on with the A68 signposted 'Edinburgh'.

3 After 2.1 kms (1.3 miles) turn right on to an unclassified road signposted 'Newbigging'. Continue for 1.5 kms (0.9 miles).

4 At Newbigging turn left at the T-junction with the A697 to Newbigging Walls.

5 At Newbigging Walls turn right on to a narrow unclassified road for a steady pull up to Burncastle. The great bulk of Dabshead Hill, 383 m (1257 ft) looks intimidating ahead.

6 After 1.5 kms (0.9 miles) at Burncastle turn right through a gate on to the rough. Go downhill then along the valley bottom on the obvious road for 0.8 kms (0.5 miles).

7 At Earnscleugh go straight on with the valley bottom road. Continue for 2.9 kms (1.8 miles).

8 The Bermuda Triangle! Turn right uphill at the T-junction beyond the cottage climbing on to true moorland.

9 Continue for 0.5 kms (0.3 miles). Keep right with the most used road. Note the many trails across the moor, but stick rigidly to the main moorland road.

10 After 1 km (0.6 miles) go through the gate then straight on, slightly left on a far lesser track. The main grouse road turns left. Initially, there are two well-defined 4-wheel-drive tracks, but these fade in the middle of the moor. Keep straight on descending towards the burn (stream) for 1.7 kms (1.1 miles).

11 At a moorland T-junction, turn left through the gate in the wall. Leave it as you find it and head for Braidshawrig.

12 There are a gate and a ford at Braidshawrig. Turn right uphill at the T-junction on the broad stony road which carries the Southern Upland Way. Go up to and beyond the trees, but then stay with the stony road beyond the summit gate.

13 After 2 kms (1.3 miles) go through the gate, then left downhill with the main track. No signposts. Continue for 1.6 kms (1 mile).

14 At Blythe farmyard at the T-junction turn left downhill, then left again with the tarmac. Continue for 1 km (0.6 miles) straight downhill.

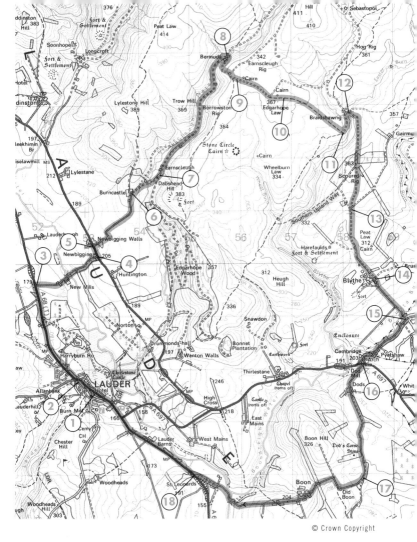

© Crown Copyright

15 Turn right at the next T-junction, no signpost. Continue for 1.4 kms (0.8 miles).

16 Turn left at the offset crossroad with the A697, take care, then right signposted 'Legerwood'. This is the final climb, long and sustained.

17 After 2.5 kms (1.5 miles) fork right towards Boon, not

signposted. Continue for 4 kms (2.5 miles). Take care on the big hill down through Boon and the ancillary dwellings, then on to Leader Water.

18 Turn right at the T-junction with the A68, not signposted and continue north to Lauder and Lauder Town Hall 2.7 kms (1.7 miles) ahead.

8 Lunan Bay

A coastal ride always has lots to offer and this route is no exception. From the bird life near Arbroath to the deserted sands of Lunan Bay this is an excellent day out. You will encounter many kinds of surfaces from woodland track and loose surfaced road to the sandy beach which is firm enough to ride at low tide.

1 Start at the east end of the Victoria Park promenade. Depart east up the ramp on to the cliff top path which is initially asphalt.

2 After 1.3 kms (0.8 miles) turn left off the path through narrow barriers at the head of a deep inlet on to a well-worn track through the fields.

3 Very shortly turn right at a field T-junction with rural twin track. Aim for the pole. Continue for 0.3 kms (0.2 miles).

4 On the cliff top path again turn left at the T-junction. You may need to walk some sections due to loose chippings. There is a little bridge among the trees, then more narrow barriers. Continue for 0.8 kms (0.5 miles).

5 Stick with the coastal path, bearing right into the wood then inland away from Carlingheugh Bay. This is a tricky single track in places with many roots and a fallen tree. Continue for 1 km (0.6 miles).

GRADE medium

DISTANCE 26.5 kms (16.5 miles)

TIME allow 3 hours

MAP OS Landranger 54 Dundee to Montrose

GRID REF AT START 658411

PARKING 100 spaces on promenade, east end of Victoria Park, Arbroath

TERRAIN gentle coastal countryside

SEASONAL SUITABILITY all year, best avoided in north-easterly gales

SURFACE cliff top path tarmac and loose surfaced and unsurfaced old coastal roads, the sands of Lunan Bay

CLIMBS/DESCENTS n/a

REFRESHMENTS none on route; pub food available in season at Auchmithie, Lunan Bay and Inverkeilor

6 Turn right at the T-junction on to a public road towards Auchmithie through a fine avenue of trees. Continue for 1.3 kms (0.8 miles).

7 At the Mains of Auchmithie go straight on around the farm. Follow the old road through the outbuildings then go east above Auchmithie.

8 Go straight on past the end of the Seafield road, eventually bearing left with the main track. Continue for 1.7 kms (1.05 miles).

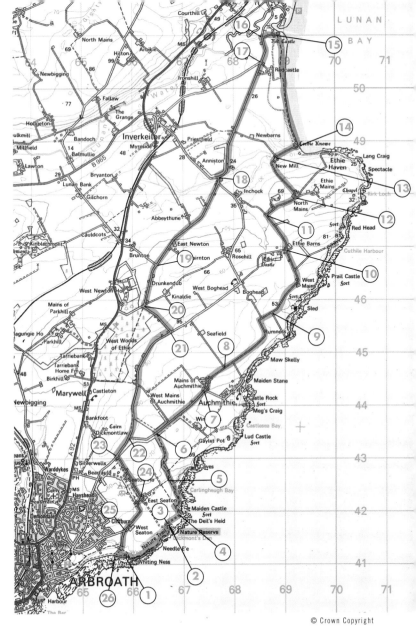

© Crown Copyright

9 Continue straight on past Rumness track, not signposted.

10 Go straight across the crossroad at Ethie Barns. Continue for 0.8 kms (0.5 miles).

11 Turn right at the tarmac signposted 'Ethie Mains'. Continue up the hill to North Mains.

12 At North Mains turn left on to a farm road then go straight on down the hill to New Mill, this is steep

and very loose in places. Continue for 1 km (0.6 miles).

13 Go straight on at the ford at New Mill towards the beach.

14 Once on the beach, turn left riding on the sand towards Red Castle for 2.3 kms (1.4 miles).

15 Turn left at Red Castle (the fort not the farm). Be prepared for a push through the soft sand of the dunes.

16 Turn left at the T-junction with the public road, not signposted.

17 Go straight on at the Redcastle crossroad, signposted 'Arbroath'. Continue for 2.5 kms (1.5 miles).

18 At Anniston, turn left across the bridge then uphill signposted 'Arbroath'. Continue for 2.2 kms (1.4 miles.)

19 Go straight on, heading towards Drunkendub.

20 Turn left at the Kinaldie crossroad signposted 'Auchmithie'.

21 Turn right at the next T-junction signposted 'Arbroath'. Continue for 2.4 kms (1.5 miles).

22 Go straight on for 0.4 kms (0.3 miles).

23 Turn left signposted 'No through road except to caravan park'. Do not enter the caravan park, keep straight on with a rougher track for 1 km (0.6 miles).

24 Turn right at the offset crossroad in East Seaton.

25 After 0.8 kms (0.5 miles) in West Seaton fork left towards the sea, not signposted.

26 Continue for 0.8 kms (0.5 miles) to Victoria Park promenade.

The woodland track inland from Carlingheugh Bay towards the Auchmithie road

9 Loch Ard

Loch Ard lies literally at the foot of the Highland Boundary Fault, the geological feature that separates the Lowlands from the Highlands. The Highlands are never more than 3 kms (2 miles) away, but this ride is designed to get you into the most beautiful places with a minimum of pain, using good forest roads.

Note: The forestry waymarkers may not always be there, or may fade in the sunlight. Rely on your map and the junction instructions.

GRADE medium

DISTANCE 19.9 kms (12.4 miles)

TIME allow 2.25 hours

MAP OS Landranger 57 Stirling and The Trossachs area

GRID REF AT START 522009

PARKING main carpark, Aberfoyle

TERRAIN gentle rolling forestry

SEASONAL SUITABILITY all year

SURFACE well made forest roads

CLIMBS/DESCENTS 1 long gentle climb/1 long gentle descent

REFRESHMENTS none on route; full facilities, Aberfoyle

1 From the main carpark in Aberfoyle turn left along the main street, the A821. May be busy in summer.

2 At the offset crossroad, turn left into Manse Road and go over the bridge, not signposted (past the back of the west carpark).

3 After 0.3 kms (0.2 miles) at Kirkton turn right at the big oak signposted 'Covenanter's Inn'. Follow the blue forestry waymarker. Continue for 1.3 kms (0.8 miles).

4 Go straight on at the offset crossroads, no waymarkers. Lochan Spling is to the right. Continue for 1 km (0.6 miles).

5 Continue straight on past a road on right following the blue waymarker.

6 After 1 km (0.6 miles) go past Gartnaul Cottage straight on past the road on the left.

7 At Duchray Castle (which is private) at a forest crossroad, bear left, uphill. Continue for 0.4 kms (0.2 miles).

8 Go straight on past a road on the left which is not marked on the Landranger map.

9 After 0.6 kms (0.3 miles) bear left with the main road over the ornamental bridge past the back entrance to Duchray Castle. Continue for 1.3 kms (0.8 miles).

10 At the T-junction turn right, downhill.

11 On reaching Bell Cottage a sign proclaims 'Things can only get worse!'. Swing left with main forest road following a blue waymarker. Continue for 1.1 kms (0.7 miles).

12 Turn right over a concrete bridge. Continue for 0.7 kms (0.4 miles).

13 At Blairvaich, keep right with main forest road. After 250 m (275 yds) there is a magnificent waterfall in a gorge through the oak woods on the right. The approach is so steep that there are ropes tied to trees to help. Not an excursion for wet weather!

14 After 1 km (0.6 miles) turn right at the T-junction and go under the aqueduct following a green waymarker.

15 At the next crossroad after 0.3 kms (0.2 miles) turn left downhill towards the white cottage. There is a red waymarker. Continue for 0.3 kms (0.2 miles).

16 Keep right, following the red waymarker.

17 Turn right before the cottages following the red waymarker. Continue for 1.9 kms (1.2 miles).

18 Turn left at the T-junction with a faded waymarker.

19 After 0.3 kms (0.2 miles) fork right then keep an eye out for

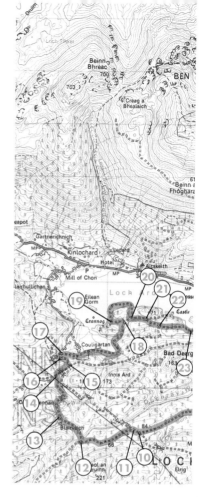

the crannog 60 m (65 yds) offshore. Skirt Loch Ard for 1.1 kms (0.7 miles).

20 Turn sharp left at the T-junction following a red waymarker.

21 After 0.3 kms (0.2 miles) fork right uphill with the main forest road.

22 After 0.3 kms (0.2 miles) keep left with main forest road following red and grey waymarkers. Continue for 0.7 kms (0.4 miles).

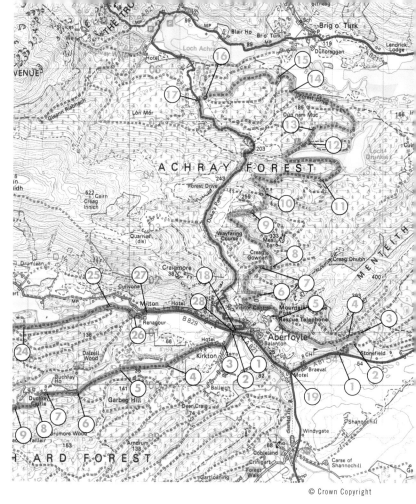

23 Keep left again following the red and grey markers. Continue for 0.3 kms (0.2 miles).

24 Go straight on past a little-used track on the left. Continue for 1.9 kms (1.2 miles) cycling near the water at times.

25 Go straight on with the main forest road and red and faded grey markers. Continue for 0.5 kms (0.3 kms).

26 At the T-junction turn left on to a very good road, then left again and down to the B829 at Milton. Stick with the obvious through road past drives and minor junctions.

27 Turn right at the T-junction in Milton onto the B829 towards Aberfoyle. Continue for 1.9 kms (1.2 miles).

28 In Aberfoyle take care at the A821. Go straight ahead. Continue for 0.1 kms (0.1 miles) to the finish.

10 Achray Forest and the Duke's Pass

A challenging ride through spectacular countryside on the geological fault line which divides the Highlands and the Lowlands. Nowhere can this division be more clearly seen than at Aberfoyle, where the mountains literally rear up behind the main street. This ride requires great effort but the rewards are worth it in terms of scenery and excitement.

1 From the Braeval carpark, depart north, uphill, through the wicket at the side of the galvanised five-bar gate.

2 After 0.4 kms (0.2 miles) bear left with the main forest road following a green forest waymarker, still going uphill. Continue for 0.2 kms (0.1 miles).

3 Turn left by another green waymarker.

4 After 0.3 kms (0.2 miles) continue straight on with a green waymarker, signposted 'Trossachs 8 miles'. Go down past the golf course. Continue for 1.6 kms (1 mile).

5 Get to Dounans Camp and keep right with the forest road signposted 'Trossachs'. Ignore the wooden walks markers – the cycle route waymarkers are mounted on plastic pipes.

6 After 1.3 kms (0.8 miles) take a hairpin turn left, at a green waymarker.

GRADE	medium
DISTANCE	26.6 kms (16.5 miles)
TIME	allow 3 hours
MAP	OS Landranger 57 Stirling and The Trossachs area
MAP REF AT START	541006
PARKING	10 spaces at Braeval carpark off A81 nr Aberfoyle
TERRAIN	steep unrelenting terrain crossing the Highland Boundary Fault twice
SEASONAL SUITABILITY	all year
SURFACE	mature forest roads and tarmac
CLIMBS/DESCENTS	2 major climbs/2 good descents
REFRESHMENTS	David Marshall Visitor Centre above Aberfoyle, café open most of the year. Fantastic view.

7 At the crossroad 1 km (0.6 miles) go straight on, uphill again following the green waymarker.

8 After 0.3 kms (0.2 miles) turn left, still uphill, still on a good forest road. Continue for 2.1 kms (1.3 miles).

9 At some barriers go straight on at the crossroad on to Forest Drive. Take care. 'Trossachs' is signposted. Continue for 0.7 kms (0.4 miles).

10 Turn left at second junction, quitting Forest Drive by a green marker. A big descent follows, loose in some places, with good views around the enormous right-hand bend.

11 After 2 kms (1.2 miles) go straight on. The track merges with Forest Drive again which skirts Loch Drunkie. Continue for 2.3 kms (1.4 miles).

12 At Loch Drunkie parking place there are toilet facilities. Go straight on for 0.2 kms (0.15 miles).

13 Go straight on at Blackwater Marshes past a road on the left. Note green and purple markers.

14 After 2.5 kms (1.5 miles) bear right with Forest Drive following green and purple waymarkers. Continue for 0.5 kms (0.3 miles).

15 Turn left uphill, quitting Forest Drive by following red and purple markers. Continue for 1.9 kms (1.2 miles).

16 At some barriers go straight on at the crossroad – back on to Forest Drive for a last few metres.

17 At the A821 turn left to start the ascent of Duke's Pass. Continue over the top to Aberfoyle 7.1 kms (4.4 miles).

A lone pine high on the initial climb over the Highland Boundary Fault

18 In Aberfoyle turn left at the T-junction still with the A821, signposted 'Stirling, Glasgow'.

19 After 1.4 kms (0.9 miles) fork left on to the A81, signposted 'Stirling'. Continue for 1 km (0.6 miles) and turn left into Braeval carpark where you started.

11 Loch Eck Circuit

The first of three rides situated on the Cowal peninsula, this is a splendid ride on a quiet winter's day, with a limited chance of snow underfoot but surrounded by high hills which will be some of the first to get a white topping. The wildlife has a definite Highland feel, you may even glimpse a golden eagle high overhead, but there are reminders of far off places too in the springtime with rhododendrons brought here from China and Tibet by the great botanist Sir Isaac Bayley Balfour.

1 Start at the Lauder Walk carpark. Return to the main forest road.

2 In Glenbranter village turn right at the offset crossroads. Lauder Cycle Trails signboards: follow the green Benmore route.

3 At the forestry workshops, bear right with the tarmac road past the green shed.

4 After 0.5 kms (0.3 miles) go straight on over the bridge, signposted Glenshellish Farm, then turn right up the hill past the farm entrance. Green (and blue) markers show the way; there is also a white post and stile at a gate.

5 Continue straight on uphill by a green waymarker, then a second confirmation post.

6 Shortly turn left, uphill again. The road swings left as it climbs then right around the crags that line the western flanks of Loch Eck. The loch will appear far below and there is a long downhill for 2.3 kms (1.4 miles).

GRADE medium
DISTANCE 31 kms (19.3 miles)
TIME allow 2.5 hours
MAP OS Landranger 56 Loch Lomond and Inverary area
PARKING 10 spaces at Lauder Walk carpark, Glenbranter, signposted from the main forest road
TERRAIN lochside circuit in a Highland environment
SEASONAL SUITABILITY all year
SURFACE good forest roads, pristine tarmac
CLIMBS/DESCENTS undulating
REFRESHMENTS café at Younger Botanic Garden, Benmore (open 15 March–31 October); Coylet Inn, Loch Eck (open all year)

7 Go straight on as a road merges from the left 2.1 kms (1.3 miles). There is a green confirmation marker and great open views down to the loch. The return route, the A851, is visible on the far side.

8 Continue straight on past a forest road on the right and downhill with a green confirmation marker. Large and small undulations.

9 After 2.8 kms (1.7 miles) continue straight on again, past

a road on the right. Take the low road by a green confirmation post.

10 At Bernice there is a gate, then go straight on past a road on the right.

11 Very shortly bear left towards the lochside with a green confirmation marker. Continue for 4.4 kms (2.7 miles) to the loch.

12 At the Water Treatment Works, go straight on past the gates on to tarmac. Continue for 1.6 kms (1 mile).

13 Go straight on at the farm and houses with the low road into substantial trees. This is the northern end of the botanic garden. No signpost or confirmation marker.

14 After 0.2 kms (0.1 miles) turn left before the turreted barn and weave down the arboretum drive. Go slowly. There is a green confirmation marker.

15 Turn left over the ornamental bridge across the River Eachaig. The café is ahead. No signpost or marker.

16 Turn left at the T-junction on to the A851 T-junction towards Strachur. Continue for 3.2 kms (2 miles).

17 Go straight on at the Coylet Inn. The road runs very close to the loch at many points. Continue for 5.3 kms (3.3 miles).

18 Go straight on at Whistlefield, signposted 'Glasgow A815'. Continue for 6 kms (3.7 miles).

19 Turn left signposted 'Glenbranter. Argyll Forest Park, Lauder'.

20 Very shortly bear left through the old gates signposted 'Lauder Walks'.

21 Turn right to the carpark 200 m (220 yds) ahead.

The first view of Loch Eck from below Creag an Adhlaic

12 Glenshellish

All three routes on the Cowal peninsula begin at Glenbranter village and have their first four directions in common. The forest roads within the Cowal Forest Enterprise woodlands are all open to bikes unless warning signs deny access due to forestry work. Please take notice of them. The Glenshellish route is a great introduction to forest riding.

1 Start at the Lauder Walks carpark. Return to the main forest road.

2 In Glenbranter village at the offset crossroad, turn right following Lauder Cycle Trails signpost. Follow the Glenshellish route, blue markers.

3 At the forestry workshops, bear right with the tarmac road past the green shed. Continue for 0.5 kms (0.3 miles).

4 Go straight on over the bridge, signposted Glenshellish Farm, then turn right uphill past the farm entrance following blue (and green) waymarkers, a white post and over the stile at the gate. This is a tough little hill, the loose surfaced road climbing between the last open fields before entering the trees.

5 After 0.3 kms (0.2 miles) fork right off the hill on to the lowest track up Glen Shellish by a blue waymarker. Continue for 4.5 kms (2.8 miles). You will ride up the east side and return down the west. Initially, there is a slight downhill then as you leave the last open field the road starts to climb. It has a good stony surface. On the skyline is Beinn Bheag 618 m (2028 ft), Meall Breac 574 m (1883 ft), and at the head of the glen Beinn Mhor 741 m (2431 ft).

6 At a ford and a forest T-junction, turn right, downhill with a blue waymarker. If the burn is in spate (flooding) retrace the route to Glenshellish Farm. The track on the west side of the glen is more susceptible to water damage. Watch out for timber reinforcing on the road, sandy washouts and holes created by water and ice.

GRADE	medium
DISTANCE	11.2 kms (7 miles)
TIME	allow 1.5 hours
MAP	OS Landranger 56 Loch Lomond and Inverary area
GRID REF AT START	110978
PARKING	10 spaces at start, Lauder Walk carpark, Glenbranter, signposted from the main forest road
TERRAIN	typical Cowal forestry
SEASONAL SUITABILITY	all year
SURFACE	forest roads
CLIMBS/DESCENTS	undulations
REFRESHMENTS	none on route

Numbers 1 to 4 (black) are common to all three rides.

7 After 3.9 kms (2.4 miles) turn right at the T-junction downhill, with a blue marker.

8 Go straight through the gate at a white house, straight on. Use the stile if it is locked.

9 At the T-junction (label no 4 on the map) turn left away from the bridge on to tarmac. Take care on the riverside road. In Glenbranter village (label 2 on the map) turn left to Lauder carpark. Continue for 0.2 kms (0.1 miles) back to the start.

The rough ford at the turn in Glen Shellish

13 Glen Branter

The shortest but most severe of the three Cowal peninsula rides, this will test the very fit and competent. The name Glen Branter comes from the 'branndair' or grid iron used for branding cattle. This area has an industrial past too, with iron furnaces situated at Inverleckan on the far side of Loch Fyne; today the village is known as Furnace.

1 Start at the Lauder Walks carpark. Return to the main forest road.

2 In Glenbranter village turn right at the offset crossroad following Lauder Cycle Trails sign board. Follow the Glenbranter route which has red markers.

3 At the forestry workshops, bear right with the tarmac road past the green shed. Continue for 0.5 kms (0.3 miles).

4 Turn right before the bridge, not signposted, following the red (and blue return) waymark, still on tarmac.

5 Keep left with the tarmac towards the white houses, not signposted. Ignore the walks post.

6 At the gate go straight on. Follow main forest road. The loose climb starts here. Ignore walks posts but obey bike prohibition signs.

7 After 0.6 kms (0.4 miles) continue straight on past a road on the left

GRADE	difficult
DISTANCE	9.3 kms (5.75 miles)
TIME	allow 1.5 hours
MAP	OS Landranger 56 Loch Lomond and Inverary area
GRID REF AT START	110978
PARKING	10 spaces at start, Lauder Walk carpark, Glenbranter, signposted from the main forest road
TERRAIN	typical Cowal forestry
SEASONAL SUITABILITY	all year
SURFACE	forest roads of varying quality, two narrow hill fords
CLIMBS/DESCENTS	2 major climbs/2 major descents
REFRESHMENTS	none on route

(this is the return track from the Glenshellish route) following a red marker.

8 Turn hairpin right uphill with the main forest road, there is a red confirmation marker.

9 Very shortly fork right on to a lower, lesser track by a red confirmation marker between the two roads. This is a far less frequented track which is bumpy, vegetated, then sandy and water worn. It starts uphill as you swing

left into Glen Branter. Two 'Dismount' warning signs appear at a very wet section, but the greatest hazard is the branches that have been laid to make the swamp passable for bigger vehicles.

10 After 2.7 kms (1.7 miles) at the end of the road, go straight on over the first ford hidden behind the bushes. Take care especially if spate (flood) conditions prevail. Pass a red confirmation marker for the return leg.

11 The second ford has a very steep approach, is narrower, and deeper. Assess the water carefully.

12 After 2.6 kms (1.6 miles) at a forest T-junction on crest, turn right on to a better road by a red confirmation marker. Continue for 1.1 kms (0.7 miles).

13 Go through the gate and at the immediate T-junction, turn right into the carpark.

The white houses near the mouth of Glen Branter. The climbing starts here!

14 Glentress

Glentress is the oldest Forestry Commission holding in south Scotland and the magnificent trees, many over 70 years' old, reflect this. The Scottish Mountain Bike Team train here and the route is for the fit and courageous only, but don't be downhearted if a super-fit person glides past, you may have been in the company of one of the best in the world.

1 Start at Glentress toll barrier. Go straight on signposted 'Carpark 0.5 mile'.

2 After 0.4 kms (0.2 miles) bear left uphill signposted 'All Traffic'.

3 Go straight on up Glen Road. (Start here if you have parked at Falla Brae.)

4 After 0.7 kms (0.4 miles) fork right into mature trees, noting a red MTB (mountain bike) waymarker.

5 Turn right into the trees on to a narrow downhill single track, across a narrow wooden bridge then straight up the bankside to a main forest road. The real mountain biking starts here!

6 At a crossroad go straight on over the main forest road, there are a 'No entry except bikes' sign and red and purple markers. The road climbs steeply and relentlessly. Continue for 0.8 kms (0.5 miles).

7 Turn left at the T-junction with Anderson Road, indicated with purple and red markers. The track continues to climb.

8 After 0.75 kms (0.5 miles) fork right by a purple marker. Within a short distance you will crest the col above Horsburgh Hope and see a road, apparently miles away contouring along the far side of the glen. That is where you are heading. Continue for 2.6 kms (1.6 miles).

GRADE	medium
DISTANCE	18.4 kms (11.4 miles)
TIME	allow 3 hours
MAP	OS Landranger 73 Peebles, Galashiels and surrounding area
GRID REF AT START	284397
PARKING	at Scottish Border Trails office, where mountain bikes can be hired, or Falla Brae carpark, beyond the Glentress toll point (50p)
TERRAIN	very hilly forest and moorland in the Upper Tweed valley
SEASONAL SUITABILITY	all year
SURFACE	mostly good forest roads, technical steep single track
CLIMBS/DESCENTS	numerous climbs/numerous descents
REFRESHMENTS	none on route

9 Turn left up a very steep loose bankside towards the Black Law col, indicated by a purple marker. The gradient soon eases, but it is still steep.

10 At Black Law col there is a wall and a T-junction. Turn left up the big hill with posts for 1.6 kms (1 mile).

11 At another col with a wall turn right towards the mast by blue markers.

12 Continue straight on with the mast road to the summit.

13 At Dunslair Heights transmission mast, 602 m (1975 ft) go straight on steeply downhill on a single track, turning left on the only track at the lower col. Blue markers show the way. Take care on the descent which is bumpy with big drops on the left.

14 After 1.9 kms (1.2 miles) turn right at the crossroad on to a good forest twin track.

15 Continue straight ahead on to a single track and a large descent. Go slowly. The track joins another forest road and turns left at the bottom.

16 After 1.5 kms (0.9 miles) go straight on around the bend past a road on the right with a blue confirmation marker.

Black Law col from Caresman Hill

17 Very shortly a road merges from left. Continue straight on with the blue marker for 0.8 kms (0.5 miles).

18 Turn left uphill over a bridge over a stream. Continue for 0.3 kms (0.2 miles).

19 Circle right above the stream on the new road, then contour the hill high above the glen.

20 After 1.9 kms (1.2 miles) the track merges with a road from left. Continue straight ahead with a blue confirmation marker.

21 Turn left at the T-junction by a blue marker.

22 Turn very sharp right on to a broad single track by blue and red markers. This is the start of the final descent.

23 After 0.3 kms (0.2 miles) turn right at the T-junction, again by blue and red markers.

24 At a huge open crossroad, turn left by red and blue markers. Continue for 0.7 kms (0.4 miles).

25 Turn right onto narrow single track. There is no warning, so look for it, you may well overshoot. This is the final descent over 1.2 kms (0.7 miles). Take care over tree roots and the little bridge.

26 The track merges with main forest road within 50 m (55 yds) of the toll point. If you started from the carpark, turn left to return.

15 Cardrona

The shortest of three Tweed rides, this places you in some of the most remote countryside abutting the Upper Tweed. It uses forest roads in the Cardrona Forest and contains technical descents which will have you hanging off the back of the bike to keep a sensible weight distribution and you will have to walk up a couple of short steep climbs.

GRADE	medium
DISTANCE	15.3 kms (9.5 miles)
TIME	allow 2.5 hours
MAP	OS Landranger 73 Peebles, Galashiels and surrounding area
GRID REF AT START	292384
PARKING	10 spaces at forest carpark Kirkburn
TERRAIN	steep Tweedside forests, exposed moorland
SEASONAL SUITABILITY	all year, subject to common sense in winter
SURFACE	forest roads, stony single track
CLIMBS/DESCENTS	1 main and 3 short very steep climbs/1 main and 1 very steep, very loose downhill
REFRESHMENTS	none on route; facilities in Innerleithen and Peebles

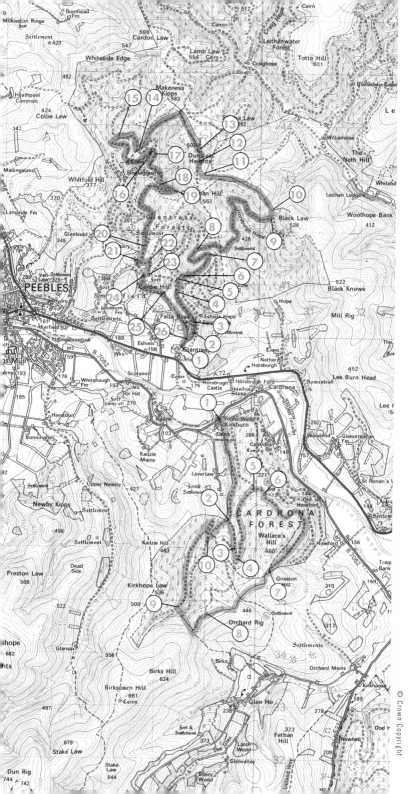

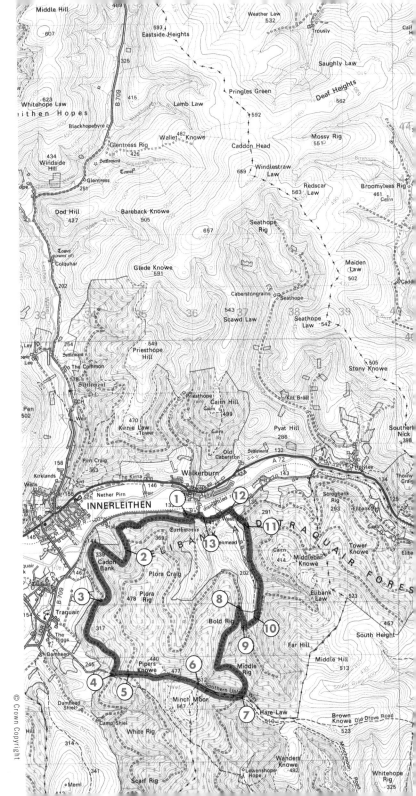

The biggest, steepest descent to Highlandshiels Burn

1 Depart south from Kirkburn carpark on Kirkburn Road. The forest road climbs gently but relentlessly for 2 kms (1.3 miles).

2 Go straight on steeply uphill with Glenpeggy Burn Road. There is a green mountain bike route confirmation waymarker.

3 After 0.6 kms (0.4 miles) go straight on past a green track on the right, not marked on the Landranger map, following a green waymarker.

4 Turn hairpin left onto Kirkburn Upper Road. Continue for 1.5 kms (0.9 miles). The road is level then descends slightly as it contours the northern slopes of Wallace's Hill.

5 Turn right up Castle Knowe South Road past a green forest waymarker.

6 After 0.3 kms (0.2 miles) fork right up Wallace Hill Road. Continue for 2.4 kms (1.5 miles). The road climbs relentlessly but provides tremendous views.

7 At the end of the forest road, go straight ahead on to high level single track. This is the southern fringe of the forest. Stick close to the boundary fence for 1.6 kms (1 mile).

8 Go straight on at an enduro (a type of track) junction past the track on the right and a green confirmation waymarker. Then turn north-west towards Highlandshiels Burn. There are two choices, the grassy track nearest the fence which is lethal when wet or the much looser stony path nearer the trees. There is a short but hellish push through head-high bracken to regain the forest road.

9 Regain the forest road after 1.1 kms (0.7 miles). Turn right at the T-junction and a green confirmation marker. Go downhill taking care at the hairpins.

10 After 2.6 kms (1.6 miles) take a hairpin left, still downhill, with the main forest road. There is a green confirmation marker. The track merges with the Kirkburn road again after 0.7 kms (0.4 miles) (label no 2 on the map). Go straight on downhill for 2.1 kms (1.3 miles) to Kirkburn carpark.

16 Elibank

A tough route for the average mountain biker with lots of continuous climbing but the scenic and downhill rewards are high. The outward leg takes quite some time but the return journey just minutes to complete. The forests of the Upper Tweed Valley give an impression of trees and nothing but trees but vistas constantly reveal themselves from the very steep hillsides.

GRADE	medium
DISTANCE	16 kms (10 miles)
TIME	allow 2 hours
MAP	OS Landranger 73 Peebles, Galashiels and surrounding area
GRID REF AT START	358367
PARKING	4 spaces at forest entrance opposite Walkerburn
TERRAIN	steep Upper Tweedside forestry and moorland
SEASONAL SUITABILITY	all year
SURFACE	good forest roads, ancient stony hill track
CLIMBS/DESCENTS	1 long climb/1 long descent
REFRESHMENTS	none on route; the Mill Shop in Walkerburn

The Minchmoor Road near the summit of the Minch Moor itself

1 Start at the forest entrance called Plora Wood, opposite the civil engineering contractors yard on the old railway. Climb east south east past the steel barrier, a board says Elibank and Traquair Forest. Follow the good forest road up the hillside for 2.3 kms (1.4 miles).

2 Go straight on past a road on the left, slightly downhill to round the nose of Cadon Bank, no signpost or waymarkers.

3 After 2.3 kms (1.4 miles) go straight on past a road on the right, uphill again following green and blue forestry bike waymarkers. Continue for 1.8 kms (1.1 miles).

4 At the crossroad turn left uphill on to the old Minchmoor Road through a dark, dense tunnel of trees, marked by a green MTB waymarker and a Southern Upland Way signpost. This section is stony and steep and can be very difficult in wet conditions. Be prepared to walk.

5 Go straight on at the next forest crossroads with the Southern Upland Way into a more open section for 1.5 kms (0.9 miles). Eventually you will break out on to open moorland which may be quite bleak and breezy.

6 At Minch Moor continue on the Southern Upland Way indicated by a signpost. Be wary of ruts and drainage traps for 1 km (0.6 miles). There is a seat and the option to climb to the summit of the Minch Moor for a picnic, if conditions are reasonable.

7 At Minch Moor col on wide open moorland turn left at the moorland crossroad on to a good forest road, then down over Middle Rig. The descent starts here and is marked by green and blue MTB (mountain bike) waymarkers.

8 After 2.4 kms (1.5 miles) turn hairpin right at the T-junction downhill for 0.5 kms (0.3 miles). The MTB confirmation post is hidden on the right.

9 Turn left downhill, the tightest option. Continue for 0.3 kms (0.2 miles).

10 Go straight on along the valley bottom road on the east side of the Bold Burn, following the MTB confirmation marker. Continue for 2.2 kms (1.4 miles)

11 Continue straight on past a road on the right. Go through the farm.

12 After 0.6 kms (0.4 miles) at a T-junction with a public road, turn left, no signpost.

13 Keep left with the hillside road to the finish.